YARDSTICKS

YARDSTICKS

Children in the Classroom Ages 4–14

3rd Edition

CHIP WOOD

Foreword by William Crain

CENTER FOR RESPONSIVE SCHOOLS, INC.

All net proceeds from the sale of this book support the work of Center for Responsive Schools, Inc., a not-for-profit educational organization and the developer of the *Responsive Classroom®* approach to teaching.

The stories in this book are all based on real events. However, to respect students' privacy, names and many identifying characteristics of students and situations have been changed.

ISBN: 978-1-892989-19-2 (paperback)
ISBN: 978-1-892989-21-5 (hard cover)

Library of Congress Control Number: 2007928775

Cover and book design by Helen Merena
Interior photographs © Peter Wrenn (unless otherwise noted). All rights reserved.
Photograph on page 219 © Joel Heaton. All rights reserved.
Interior motif photographs by Paula Denton, Andy Dousis, Peter Wrenn, and Cherry Wyman.

Thanks to all the families who allowed us to use their children's artwork and photos on the cover and within this book.

Center for Responsive Schools, Inc.
85 Avenue A, P.O. Box 718
Turners Falls, MA 01376-0718

800-360-6332
www.responsiveclassroom.org

Eleventh printing 2017

For Reenie

---

and to Jackie Haines,
my mentor in child
development

Contents

ix   Foreword

xiii   Preface to the Third Edition

3   Introduction

11   Developmental Considerations

39   Yardsticks: Broad Guidelines

47   Four-Year-Olds

57   Five-Year-Olds

73   Six-Year-Olds

85   Seven-Year-Olds

97   Eight-Year-Olds

107   Nine-Year-Olds

119 Ten-Year-Olds

131 Eleven-Year-Olds

143 Twelve-Year-Olds

155 Thirteen-Year-Olds

167 Fourteen-Year-Olds

183 Acknowledgments

185 References

195 APPENDIX A: The Birthday Cluster Exercise
Where Is Your Class Developmentally?

201 APPENDIX B: Resources for Educators

207 APPENDIX C: Resources for Parents

209 APPENDIX D: Some Favorite Books for
Children at Different Ages

Foreword

E ducation reform has become a top priority in the United States. Our political and corporate leaders constantly press for higher academic standards and more rigorous standardized tests to ensure that students will be prepared for the new global economy. To advance this agenda, policymakers have created a host of other initiatives, including efforts to align public education with specific workforce needs and penalties for schools that fail to raise test scores.

But, as educator Jeffrey Kane has observed,* these plans and policies typically leave something out: the child. The child is more than a test score or a future worker. Every child is a full, living individual with his or her own needs, interests, fears, and desires. And although educators must concern themselves with the child's future success, the child is very much a person in the present moment.

It might seem that a focus on the child's present life is a luxury today, when there is so much talk about preparing students for the competitive, high-tech world they will enter when they are grown. But a focus on the present is at the heart of the developmental perspective in education. In this view, children are inwardly motivated to develop different capacities at different stages, and we must give them opportunities to perfect their naturally emerging capacities at their present stage. If, instead, we simply focus on the skills they will need later on, we may curtail their full development.

*Kane, Jeffrey. 1995. "Educational Reform and the Dangers of Triumphant Rhetoric." In *Educational Freedom for a Democratic Society*. Ron Miller, Ed. Brandon, Vermont: Resource Center for Redesigning Education.

For example, young children have an especially strong urge to develop the artistic and imaginative sides of their personalities. And given a chance, they develop their creative capacities in breathtaking ways. But today's educational policymakers, with their eyes on the future economy, are replacing artistic and imaginative activities with academic skills at very early ages. As a result, children miss out on the chance to develop their full potentials.

Educators who respect the child's own developmental schedule will find Chip Wood's book, *Yardsticks*, immensely rewarding. For each age, from four to fourteen years, Wood gives us a rich account of the child's naturally emerging capacities and distinctive ways of learning. Wood recognizes that not all children at each chronological age are exactly the same, but he provides useful guideposts that will help teachers select developmentally appropriate tasks and activities. For example, Wood cautions against burdening four-year-olds with paper-and-pencil tasks and reminds us of their need for physical activity. He also points out that seven-year-olds are eager to learn how mechanical things work, ten-year-olds delight in facts and memorization, and young teenagers often work best in social groups. For each age, Wood provides a treasure trove of useful observations and insights.

Wood incorporates ideas from Jean Piaget and Erik Erikson, but his primary inspiration is the work of Arnold Gesell. Like Gesell, Wood wants us to appreciate the uneven nature of development— how children go through periods of disequilibrium as well as periods of harmonious functioning. This knowledge helps us become more patient and understanding with children. More broadly, Wood shares Gesell's ability to write simply and express simple but powerful truths. For example, Wood reminds us that "the whole child goes to school; therefore, decisions about physical activity, food policies, and the development of social and emotional skills are as important as curriculum choices and test results."

Wood is also very aware of recent insights into the cultural lives of children. I believe readers will find much to interest them in his discussions of the strengths of African American and Latino/Hispanic children and their families.

Throughout the book, Wood demonstrates a love of childhood and a gentle sense of humor. He entertains us with many anecdotes. My favorite is about a five-year-old boy who marches up to his kindergarten teacher's desk, places his hands on his hips, and announces, "You don't seem to understand, teacher; I just came here to eat and play!" The boy's proclamation speaks of both his pluck and his naiveté. He has no idea of the force of the standards movement that is about to crash down upon him. But his spirited defense of his interests is admirable, as is Wood's defense of the interests of all children.

William Crain
Professor of Psychology
The City College of New York

Preface to the Third Edition

Yardsticks is about children in American classrooms. It presents common characteristics of children's physical, social, emotional, language, and cognitive development at each age from four through fourteen. The book also suggests classroom activities and curriculum focuses appropriate for each age, based on those common developmental characteristics.

Since the first edition of *Yardsticks* was published thirteen years ago, it has captured the attention of educators in other countries. In this edition, therefore, I wanted to clarify that I am not speaking for what might be appropriate practices in classrooms universally, but, rather, to the particular cultural context of American schools. This is not to say that American classrooms have not become more culturally diverse over the last thirteen years, for they certainly have.

Despite this increasing multiculturalism, however, it's important to remember that no two countries or cultures offer the same educational context to their children. Thus, even though, broadly speaking, children the world over may share common developmental stages, the schooling implications of these stages will vary from culture to culture. This book suggests the implications of children's developmental stages for the teaching taking place in American classrooms.

Since the late 1990s, the trend in U.S. education has been toward more curriculum standardization and more standardized testing. I and many other educators worry deeply about this trend—about the damage we are doing to our children when we force upon them a way of schooling that runs counter to what they are capable of doing and how they naturally learn at each age. In this edition, therefore, I make a stronger argument for educators to pay attention to children's developmental abilities and characteristics in this age of standards-driven schooling.

The previous edition included a brief section on African American children's development; this edition adds a comparable section on Latino/Hispanic children. Although we need to be educated about all the cultural groups in our schools, this book addresses these two groups because they are the largest minorities in America. In each of these sections I give an overview of some cultural and linguistic matters that are important to consider alongside the broader developmental issues that are the primary subject of this book.

As in earlier editions, the section on African American children in this edition draws on the work of Janice E. Hale-Benson. Her latest book, *Learning While Black: Creating Educational Excellence for African American Children* (Hale-Benson 2001), is a clarion call for educators and parents in the African American community. Yet it is much more: It is a model for the kind of learning community every American should want in every school.

For understanding of Latino/Hispanic cultural considerations in schooling, I am indebted to the work of Iliana Reyes at the University of Arizona. Her ongoing research on the literacy, social, and cognitive development of bilingual preschoolers from Mexican families in America, one of the largest sectors of the U.S. Latino/Hispanic population, has been invaluable.

Certainly, there are factors besides race and ethnicity that affect children's interactions in school and the larger world. Economic class is a prime example. While this book will not go into how poverty or wealth affects children's development, I do want to acknowledge the importance of economics in children's lives. As a principal in a disadvantaged rural school, I see the challenges that poverty presents in the classroom every day. As educators, we would be wise to educate ourselves about what poverty means in the lives of children. Much good information can be found at the websites of Columbia University's National Center for Children in Poverty (www.nccp.org) and the University of Wisconsin's Institute for Research on Poverty (www.irp.wisc.edu).

As you use this book, I ask that you please pay attention to the limits of developmental characteristics and characterizations. Such general expectations help us gain an appreciation for the patterns of development, but they are not precise predictions of what will happen at a given age. Culture, environment, health, temperament, and personality all affect the make-up of every child at every age. It's helpful that certain patterns have emerged and been documented, but they are never absolute. As Melvin Konner writes in *Childhood: A Multicultural View*, "We have to be patient; we are finding out new things just as fast as we know how. And if anyone gives you the impression that he has the answers now to the great timeless questions about childhood, you can smile and listen politely or you can turn your back and walk away, but in any case don't believe him" (Konner 1993, 20–21).

I want to be clear that this book is not a definitive work, but rather a collection of snapshots of children's development. These snapshots are based on observations in the classroom—mine and those of many other educators—and the observations of many researchers and theorists at different points in our educational history. As useful as these snapshots are, full understanding can be obtained only in the context of your own search for meaning about children's growth and development.

I am sure most of you are captivated, as I am, by the magic and mysteries of childhood. I also share with you a deep and abiding reverence for children's clear, honest vision of their world—how they perceive and interact with the world at different stages of their growth. I believe it is our duty to protect and nourish their vision through our teaching and parenting. I hope *Yardsticks* helps you in this effort. Working together, we can keep childhood alive and learning an adventure.

Robert (Chip) Wood
Buckland, Massachusetts
2007

*"How old would you be if you
didn't know how old you were?"*

ATTRIBUTED TO SATCHEL PAIGE

―――――

*"In order to be treated fairly and equally,
children have to be treated differently."*

MELVIN KONNER, *CHILDHOOD: A MULTICULTURAL VIEW*

YARDSTICKS

Introduction

The need to understand and honor children's development is greater today than ever. At the beginning of the twenty-first century, American educational culture is dominated by a growing uniformity in curriculum content, ever-increasing amounts of instructional time spent on assessment, and the expectation (driven by state and federal mandates) that children will master subject area content and skills at younger and younger ages.

Such trends do not bode well for children. They do not educate the whole child, support well-rounded growth, or inspire children's excitement for learning, and they seem to add undue stress for students and teachers. Further, while the current standards-driven education isn't good for any child, it is especially problematic for those who have immigrated recently from Somalia, Southeast Asia, Eastern Europe, Mexico, and many other parts of the world. These children are required to master English and curriculum content well enough to take mandated state tests within a year of entering American schools.

Leaving Childhood Behind?

As a result of these trends, and in a political era in which national educational law and policy is dubbed "No Child Left Behind," we are in grave danger of leaving childhood behind. Sadly, our classrooms have returned to an almost singular focus on the core three r's of readin', ritin', and 'rithmetic and we're in a period of endless testing of these skills, almost to the exclusion of critical social, cultural, and civic learning. Some call it the age of accountability.

Test data are certainly relevant to child development and education, but testing is best when used in moderation, and only in relationship to the child's developing capacity to cognitively and emotionally tolerate testing. In our rush to "fix" our schools, we are supplanting essential aspects of childhood education—imagination, play, creativity, scientific curiosity, reading for pleasure—with testing in every subject. Recess and special area subjects such as art and music, world languages, and even computer literacy are held hostage to subjects that are measured by standardized state assessments.

This is not the first time we've seen this sort of imbalance in American education. Over the last fifty years or so, we've seen two earlier attempts to fix children's learning in the way we are seeing it tried now—by making all children fit a preset curriculum that largely ignores developmental considerations, rather than making curriculum fit children's developmental needs. The first such period was after the Russian Sputnik launch in 1957, when we feared falling behind in the race to space.

That "space race" period ended in the 1960s with the "open classroom" era, which used a more child-centered approach to teaching. In the 1970s, as we struggled to keep up with the Japanese and other global economic competitors, the pendulum swung back toward a singular focus on straight academics, beginning as early as preschool and kindergarten. In the 1980s and early 1990s, there was a pushback from the field of early childhood education, which reintroduced "developmentally appropriate programs" into American public and private education.

Amid the cycling of educational trends, it's important to remember that the long-term answer to a stronger, more robust, and more rigorous education for all children, as most everyone who

spends time observing children in classrooms knows, is better teachers. The most skilled I have worked with over my career have been those who have known what is appropriate for their students from a developmental point of view.

As these good teachers have demonstrated, knowing curriculum content is one thing; knowing children and child development, quite another. Most teachers receive one course in child development (at best) during their education studies. Their second course is on-the-job training through their own direct observations and comparisons of children from year to year, age to age in the grade or grades that they teach.

Year after year, teachers have told me this book has confirmed what they have seen on their own or has helped them make sense of their observations. It has given them confidence to stick with their most deeply held beliefs about what is right for children. I hope the book will continue to serve that purpose.

My Own Journey

In 1978, after my first six years as an elementary school teacher and teaching principal, I attended a workshop on child development sponsored by Gesell Institute. That one day changed forever my view of education. Like many of you who are now struggling with questions about whether testing and other educational trends are really helping us teach our children, I was then struggling with the "back-to-basics" trend of the 1970s, which did not make sense to me. I worried about negative consequences as we pushed our academic expectations down onto younger and younger children.

In the Gesell workshop, I began to have my concerns confirmed as I learned to see the children for who they were, for the lives to be lived, not just the lessons to be learned. I began to see the contextual nature of learning reading and math as I learned to appreciate the developmental understanding children bring to subject matter at different ages. I vowed to learn more. Over the past twenty-nine years I have focused my professional efforts toward understanding the relationship between development and schooling in American classrooms and passing this information on to teachers and parents.

In 1985, with my colleagues Ruth Sidney Charney, Marlynn K. Clayton, Marion Finer, and Jay Lord, I helped write the first book published by Northeast Foundation for Children (NEFC), *A Notebook for Teachers: Making Changes in the Elementary Curriculum* (NEFC 1985/1993). In that book I charted the developmental characteristics of children from ages five to seven, using the work of Arnold Gesell, Jean Piaget, and Erik Erikson as primary references. Since then, I have broadened my knowledge through direct observation in diverse classrooms and through study of the works of current experts in child development.

In 1999, as part of my book *Time to Teach, Time to Learn: Changing the Pace of School*, I wrote three narrative chapters based on my observations of children in both primary and middle school grades. Taken together, the narratives paint a detailed picture of the conflict between children's developmental needs and the time pressures of most school environments today, even in classrooms with excellent teachers. Those who wish to read more deeply about the school lives of children may find these three chapters useful.

My memories of my own childhood, my classroom work, and the years spent raising my own children help me see childhood with the eyes of a child, a teacher, a principal, and a parent; and now, watching my grandchildren provides daily action research! My approach to understanding child development is a mixture of theory and practice, reading and observation, reflection and writing.

Today's Students and Teachers

The U.S. school-age population continues to grow more diverse culturally and linguistically. African American and Latino/Hispanic students, especially, are accounting for larger and larger percentages of the student population. In 1972, African American students constituted 14.8 percent of students in grades K–12 and Latino/Hispanic students, 6.0 percent. In 2004, those percentages were 16.0 and 19.3, respectively. In 1972, European American students accounted for 77.8 percent of our K–12 population; in 2004, that percentage was 57.4 (U.S. Department of Education 2006).

Other ethnic and cultural groups have grown during the past thirty-odd years as well. From 1972 to 2004, the percentage of children who were Asian and Pacific Islander quadrupled, to 4.1 percent, and the children who were in other cultural categories more than doubled, to 3.2 percent (U.S. Department of Education 2006). Children in American classrooms will continue to become a culturally richer and more diverse population long into the country's future.

Given these trends, it's more crucial than ever that we diversify the teaching force to keep some semblance of pace with the changes, and that all of us working in schools know children not only individually and developmentally, but culturally, too. How children see the world and how they think and act at school is affected by their developmental differences, but also by the family cultures and values they bring to the classroom. A combination of a diversified teacher population and a valuing of all children's home cultures by all teachers will ensure a rich and equitable education for all children.

Nurturing Children at Home and at School

Teachers tell me how comforting and useful *Yardsticks* is for them as they learn about a new group of children every year. Most teachers have an abiding belief in the goodness of children and in

children's willingness to learn, but sometimes a child's behavior or learning style is a puzzle. Thinking first about common developmental characteristics for a child at that age can be helpful. It can remind teachers that some of what they are seeing is natural and to be expected of children that age. Alternatively, if what they are seeing is not typical for that age, they can then ask for more detailed assessments and observations by specialists.

Teachers also use the information in this book to set up their physical classrooms at the beginning of the school year, to think about their schedules and how long children can sit still without a break at different ages, and to compare their state-issued curriculum expectations to children's typical interests and approaches to learning at different ages.

Parents have told me that *Yardsticks* has been one of the books they turn to when their child is going through a particularly hard time. It often reminds them that the behavior worrying them is, in fact, pretty common and that many other parents with children of the same age are being confronted by the same issues. The book also points out the joys of each age, lest we miss them!

Yardsticks often provides a common starting point from which teachers and parents can begin communicating about a child as a whole person, a person with intellectual, social and emotional, physical, and language strengths and needs. With this awareness, we can all do a better job of continually nurturing the children in our care.

Learning More about Child Development

The information about children's age-by-age developmental characteristics in this book is based largely on classical Western child development research done beginning in the early 1900s. Jean Piaget, Arnold Gesell, Maria Montessori, Lev Vygotsky, Erik Erikson, Rudolph Steiner, Caroline Pratt, Lucy Sprague Mitchell, Dorothy Cohen, Louise Bates Ames, and others have contributed to form a rich body of knowledge about how children grow and learn. The works of many of these child development experts are listed in the References section. Most of these seminal works, however, share a common limitation, being largely focused on the European American world of middle class children. Also, at between fifty and 100 years old, the works are dated. Nonetheless, without this research, it is hard to imagine where the field of child development would be today.

The reference list also provides more up-to-date resources, particularly those I have found useful in writing about the cultural context of development in American classrooms today. Barbara Rogoff's book *Apprenticeship in Learning* (Rogoff 1990) was important to earlier editions of this book, and her later book, *The Cultural Nature of Human Development* (Rogoff 2003), is significant for this revised edition. In her new work, Rogoff writes, "human development is a process of people's changing participation in sociocultural activities of their communities" (Rogoff 2003, 52). As I have seen clearly in American classrooms over and over, the social, emotional, and cultural development of which Rogoff speaks is as critical to learning as language, cognitive, and physical development.

Developmental Considerations

Four Principles of Child Development

As educators, parents, and others who observe children know, children tend to share common patterns of growth. Those patterns may vary somewhat in expression, depending on the country and culture in which the children live. But physically, socially, emotionally, in their ability to think, and in their ability to understand and use language, children largely move in similar ways through the ages of childhood and the stages of development.

In the first half of the last century, the so-called "giants" in the field of child development—people such as Jean Piaget, Arnold Gesell, Maria Montessori, Erik Erikson, and Lev Vygotsky—observed, researched, and recorded most of the developmental patterns that form the basis of our knowledge of how children mature. Each of these experts looked at the whole spectrum of children's development in the journey toward adulthood, though today each is often noted for work in one key area. Gesell, for instance, is noted for his work on physical milestones; Piaget, for cognition; and Erikson, for social and emotional growth.

Over the years, the patterns in physical, social, emotional, cognitive, and language growth that these experts identified have been corroborated by parents and teachers through their own experience of teaching and parenting children at different ages.

At the beginning of the twenty-first century, four key principles about child growth and development have stood the test of time:

1. Children's physical maturation, language acquisition, social and emotional behavior, cognition, and ways of approaching the world follow reasonably predictable patterns. These patterns have been broken down into stages in different ways according to particular theories.

2. Children generally go through predictable stages in the same order, but they will not all go through them at the same rate. Important details in their development are deeply influenced by culture, personality, and environment. No two children are the same, no two families, no two communities, no two schools.

   If, for example, we compare two ten-year-olds, even within a single culture, we may find that one child is more like a typical nine-year-old in some developmental aspects, and another is more like a typical eleven-year-old in those same aspects. This developmental span (from nine to eleven) is not necessarily a cause for concern, as long as each child's growth is relatively even and not dramatically delayed or erratic. Thus a child's chronological age may not be the same as his or her developmental age: If a child is chronologically ten but behaves more like most nine-year-olds, and this behavior lasts more than three months or so after turning ten, this child is most likely still developmentally nine, and parents and teachers should take that fact into consideration.

3. The various aspects of development do not proceed at the same rate. A youngster who matures quickly in cognitive areas may

mature slowly in physical and social ones. A child who advances slowly in cognitive areas may demonstrate above average physical and social abilities. Ability in music, mechanical tasks, or the arts may develop more quickly or slowly than language acquisition or the ability to perform academic tasks in school.

4. Growth is uneven. Like the seasons, the tides, the turning of Earth on its axis and around the sun, the birth and death of stars, the music of the universe—there is an ebb and flow to life that is mystical and spiritual as well as natural. Babies are calm at one time of day, fretful at another. Children are more easygoing at one age, more resistant at others. Learning seems to come in spurts followed by periods of consolidation. Obvious periods of sudden physical growth are often followed by periods of little notable physical change. This shifting back and forth is part of the life cycle and appears to continue into adulthood. Changes are quite marked during infancy, in both rate and degree; become less dramatic during much of adulthood; and are again marked during the elder years.

Developmental Needs in American Classrooms

The four developmental concepts just discussed should guide decisions we make in our country about schooling. We need to attend to all areas of growth because each plays a crucial role in learning outcomes and in providing balance in a child's life. The whole child goes to school; therefore, decisions about physical activity, food policies, and the development of social and emotional skills are as important as curriculum choices and test results. A majority of American schools, however, increasingly shortchange children's overall developmental needs in favor of lopsided attention to cognitive development as expressed through standards–based academic assessment.

As an example of this lopsidedness, elementary school schedules in the United States are now largely governed by directives requiring ninety minutes of time-on-task instruction each day in each core academic content area, regardless of the age or grade of the students. Since the late 1990s, the educational trend has also been to give teachers less leeway in deciding on the structure and content of the school day. More schools have returned to the single-grade classrooms common in earlier decades, and increasingly more time is spent throughout the school year on paper-and-pencil assessments, detracting from actual teacher instruction time. Time is increasingly limited for physical, social, emotional, and cultural development, as evidenced by reductions in recess, physical education, art, music, theatre, and even integrated, theme-based academic units. For teachers and students, the world of instruction has returned to a more narrow and prescribed textbook-dependent, workbook-focused orientation typical of other "academics only" cycles during the past fifty years.

In the ten years since the last edition of this book, much has changed in the world of education, and in the amount of exposure children have to the world through the constant barrage of electronic media. But children's development has not changed. Children still follow the same patterns of development they have for generations. The pages ahead offer information about child development that can help teachers and parents advocate for the timeless developmental needs and rights of children as they go to school.

Children's Physical Needs

FOOD AND WATER

All children have a need for food beyond three square meals a day. Schools should pay attention to this because hunger is an educational issue. Making sure that children have enough food and water when they need it contributes to healthy physical growth and effective learning. Early childhood educators have long recognized this and have built time into the school day for preschool, kindergarten, and early primary grade children to have a snack in addition to breakfast and lunch. But why stop at the primary grades? We know that children of all ages benefit from having snacks during their school day, and that lack of a snack contributes to poor attention, concentration, and attitude. Unfortunately, snack usually ends in first or second grade, replaced with the rule: NO FOOD OR DRINK ALLOWED IN THE CLASSROOM.

Some teachers do tell children and parents that snack is allowed and that they can bring something from home. This doesn't have to be a big production. Something as simple as a piece of fruit or some pretzels can ease a child's hunger. Many teachers even keep a stash of pretzels in the closet for students to share. (The one thing to discourage is bringing or offering sweets and junk food, which can contribute to excess nervous energy and obesity in children.)

I'm aware that in our current extremely time-conscious school environment, stopping the whole class for snack may seem unacceptable to some schools. But there are alternatives. Teachers can set up a snack table in one area of the room and allow children to regulate their own eating. This not only eliminates an interruption to lessons, but can create an opportunity for children to learn about nutrition as well as respectful and caring behavior around the snack table. Snack can then become an integral part of the social and academic curriculum.

Children need water during the school day perhaps even more than they need food. Water allows the body and brain to function well. A child who's not drinking enough water may get a headache, become dizzy, or feel very tired (Mayo Clinic 2007). These are hardly ideal conditions for concentrating on schoolwork! Because children's bodies may already be slightly dehydrated by the time they feel thirsty (Mayo Clinic 2006, 2007), teachers and parents should encourage children to drink water regularly, especially when they're active and in hot weather. Children at school should be allowed not only to "go get a drink" but also to bring water bottles from home.

The developmental issue is clear: Food and water are major ingredients in meeting growing children's daily needs. Given that a child's inability to pay attention may be rectified by a simple snack or a drink of water, it is extraordinarily shortsighted to prevent students from eating healthy snacks and drinking plenty of water in school. Whether you're a parent or educator, the next time you pick up that mid-morning cup of coffee, think about the food and water policy at school. Parents can talk about this issue with teachers, the food service director, and the principal at PTO meetings. Administrators can find out what snacks are available from breakfast and lunch programs. Teachers can advocate for pro-snack and water policies and be sure to provide opportunities for snack and water during the school day.

EXERCISE

I am amazed at the number of schools I have visited where a short morning or afternoon recess is a thing of the past. Children who get even twenty minutes of outdoor play in the middle of each day are the lucky ones. According to the American Association for the Child's Right to Play, an estimated forty percent of all elementary schools have either eliminated or are in the process of eliminating recess (American Association for the Child's Right to Play).

Formal physical education classes have also been reduced to as little as a half hour a week in some elementary schools. Policymakers say they have taken these severe measures because there is just too much work to do in school and not enough time to do it.

Policies such as these will not help children learn more. Just as they need food and water more often than at mealtimes, all children need frequent exercise. While benefiting the body, exercise also delivers oxygen to the brain, and nine-year-olds need that oxygen just as much as four-year-olds. In fact, many discipline problems in school can be traced directly to lack of physical activity. This is especially true for the growing numbers of children with ADD (attention deficit disorder), ADHD (attention deficit hyperactivity disorder), or ODD (oppositional defiance disorder). These children desperately need physical release in their school day. Their academic proficiency and social competence will rise with an increase in physical education, not with more time spent doing sedentary paper-and-pencil activities.

In some places, children are kept indoors because administrators say they can't guarantee children's safety on the playground. The "weather forecast" approach is common as well. A few degrees too cold or too hot or a prediction of light rain or fine mist can bring the announcement over the intercom: "Teachers are advised that there will be indoor recess today." But indoor recess is a poor substitute for outdoor time. Sunlight and air are as important to human growth as to the growth of plants and trees. Spending all day in school buildings, sometimes with poor ventilation and inadequate lighting, is counterproductive to optimum learning. Parents and teachers should insist that children spend time outside at least twice a day. This is especially important in school buildings without windows. Even a five- or ten-minute break to run around the school building or jump rope in the side yard can make a huge difference in the way children feel and perform in the classroom.

On days when children must stay inside the classroom, a break to do "Head and Shoulders, Knees and Toes," aerobics to music, or five minutes of the latest dance craze can improve attention and attitude. Teachers need the physical exercise, too. Oxygen flowing to our brains helps keep us cheerful and engaging, and that is good not only for us, but also for the children.

How Schools Use Time

ORGANIZING THE SCHOOL DAY

Many years ago, the brilliant educator Sylvia Ashton-Warner described the daily rhythms of classroom life in her classic book, *Teacher* (Ashton-Warner 1963). Simply and poetically, she wrote about how children need times to "breathe in" and "breathe out" as they go through the school day. She believed that children will learn as naturally as they breathe if we pay attention to their needs when planning and pacing our instruction.

But schedules in today's American schools don't always pay attention to the pace of childhood or children's changing developmental needs from age to age. Consider, for instance, the long-held practice of scheduling recess right after lunch. Haven't we got it backwards? Doesn't it make more sense to work up an appetite on the playground and then eat a good, healthy lunch, rather than to eat as quickly as possible and run right out to play on a full stomach? Schools that have reorganized their schedules to allow for the simple change of putting recess before lunch have seen improvements in the children's afternoon behaviors and energy levels.

Regardless of whether they put recess or lunch first, many schools next push the children right into the afternoon's instruction, with no "breathing out" time. Not surprisingly, this hard-driving shape of the day common in so many schools mimics that of the larger adult world. In our classrooms, the lack of a midday break often makes the afternoon a downhill journey of inattention and listlessness, with the children focusing on the moment of dismissal. Offering a quiet time after lunch, during which children can experience a few moments of precious silence in the classroom reading, drawing, writing, or resting by themselves can energize their brains and refresh their spirits. The afternoon can then be a learning-filled adventure.

Closely related to the order of school activities is the pace of them—how much time we allow for each activity before moving on to the next—and the manner in which we move the children on. Eight years ago, I wrote in my book *Time to Teach, Time to Learn: Changing the Pace of School* about the "absolutely inappropriate pace of teaching and learning which daily decreases the quality of education and the very quality of life for millions of children during their school years" (Wood 1999, i). My concern has only grown. Children have almost no time in their school day to reflect on their learning, to make calm, organized transitions between classes or subjects, or to delve deeply into learning that they love. Sadly, school resembles more and more a miniature adult world of packed schedules, multitasking, and exhaustion. Not only are we modeling this world for children by our own adult behavior, we are moving these practices into the world of school with the belief that they are necessary for children's academic success.

That belief is completely mistaken. The fact is that children do not experience time the way adults do. Their understanding of past, present, and future is undeveloped in early childhood and becomes more sophisticated as they mature into adolescence. Therefore, although high school and college students may switch from one class or assignment to another relatively easily, younger children cannot. This means, first of all, that elementary children should not be shuffled from one classroom to another, one teacher to another, in a way that chunks their day up into short periods. This is especially true in preschool, kindergarten, and primary grades, when one of the most important variables for academic success, educational experts say, is the constant attention of a single teacher with whom the child can develop not only a predictable and meaningful relationship but also a consistent understanding of expectations about time constraints. This single teacher can guide children in making transitions, finishing assignments, and eventually in completing and bringing in homework and planning their own time wisely.

Elementary students' relative difficulty in switching from one task to another also means that when we must move children on to a new task, classroom, or teacher, we must do it in a calm, unhurried way. Hurrying children leads them to feel excessive frustration and anxiety. "Hurry up, children, it's time for gym; hurry up, children, it's time for spelling; hurry up, children, it's time for music." This way of talking can only add anxiety for children who are probably already feeling rushed. Early childhood expert Jackie Haines tells the story of one kindergarten teacher who knew she'd had enough when she heard herself say, "Hurry up children, it's time to rest" (Personal communication).

Contrast this with a calm reminder or direction to children to be mindful of the time. For a seven-year-old, a quiet individual reminder can make all the difference in the world. "Don't forget, we have gym in five minutes. Now's the time to clean up." In kindergarten, a gentle bell sounds and the teacher says, "In five minutes we will be ending our working period. Think about what you need to do to be finished." It's important in our distracted adult world to remember that children become deeply absorbed in the important business of learning and growing. We need to help them manage this process rather than drag them helter-skelter through a hectic day.

Older children in grades four through eight, like younger students, love to be absorbed in their learning and do well with

block scheduling and lots of project-related work. But adults expect these older children to demonstrate increasing efficiency in their management of time—time for homework, sports, extracurricular activities, taking care of younger siblings at home. As the expectations intensify, not having enough time can be a constant worry or complaint heard from these "tweeners" and young adolescents. Teachers can help by checking assignments with each other so that, for instance, big tests in several subjects are not scheduled on the same day, or by providing "homework passes" when they notice individual students overloaded or know they are dealing with a significant health or family issue.

For adolescents, an additional time-related issue that affects learning is their sleep schedule. Sleep research in recent years has shown that adolescents do better when allowed to follow their natural circadian rhythms of sleeping later and staying up later. Even a small adjustment in the school schedule, such as starting middle school an hour later than elementary (rather than the usual other way around) may make a big difference in how adolescents perform in school. Indeed, such adjustments are critical not only to adolescents' school success but to their basic health and safety as well. Results of a major National Institutes of Health study published by the National Sleep Foundation found that adolescents are showing increased signs of sleep deprivation and reliance on stimulants to make their way through their demanding school days (National Sleep Foundation 2000).

THE SCHOOL CALENDAR

As American society changes, the school calendar is coming under increased scrutiny. Most schools still use the agrarian calendar, which worked well when the major considerations of family and community life were planting and harvesting. But there is little question that this calendar is impractical in American society today and, in fact, works against children's academic growth and development. Most schools in the United States operate on a 180-day calendar. Does it make sense, when curricula are so crowded and most families no longer farm, that children spend half a year in school and half a year out?

Simply lengthening the school year may not raise academic achievement, but achievement likely will result from a combination of increasing the amount of in-school time and adjusting the way that time is used. There has been some change in recent years: In 2006 the National Association for Year-Round Education counted over 3,000 schools in the United States, Canada, and the Pacific Rim that had extended the school day and year in some way (National Association for Year-Round Education 2006).

Schools exploring extended school time (either through longer school days or by adding more school days to the calendar year) have a unique opportunity to consider adapting the pace of daily learning to match the developmental tempo of the children in their classrooms. Under continuing governmental pressure to raise achievement scores, however, schools may just add time in hopes that the quantity of instruction will improve the quality of children's education. That would be a mistake. Instead, I hope that we'll keep in mind our increasing understanding of child development and the value of giving children the time and pacing they need to learn at their best. Then we will be able to build new school calendars, schedules, and programs that truly benefit children.

Grouping Students

"What grade are you in?" is the student version of the adult conversation starter, "What do you do?" Children from different schools love to compare notes about what they are studying, the books they are reading, what they do in physical education, how much time they have for recess, and what lunch is like at their grade level. Grade level is a big topic for teachers and administrators as well: Educators are continuously puzzling over the question of how to group students in ways that are beneficial for children and practical for teachers.

From the days of the one-room schoolhouse, American educators have tried many ways to do this grouping. Most American elementary schools today use the single-grade, separate-classroom structure. In this structure, all the children with birthdays between certain cut-off dates are assigned to a grade level (first, second, third, etc.) and spend one year with only classmates of the same grade and with a teacher, and perhaps support teachers, who teach only that grade. This certainly is not the only way to group students, however. During various periods of the last century, American public schools have tried alternatives that involve grouping children of different ages or different grades together, though none have become long-term, mainstream approaches.

Yet there's much to be said for these alternative methods of organizing schools if the methods take into consideration children's developmental stages. Mixed-age and mixed-grade groupings give children increased opportunities to learn with others who are reaching similar developmental milestones in the physical, social, emotional, cognitive, and language realms. They also give older and younger children opportunities to learn from—and teach—one another.

Related to mixing ages and grades is looping, in which a teacher stays with a group of children as they progress to the next grade, and then loops back to begin teaching a new group of students at

the younger grade. The advantages of extending children's time with one teacher include an increased sense of stability for children, more student persistence with academic tasks, and a stronger curriculum thread with less repetition of material (Nichols 2002, Elliot and Capp 2003). Teachers come to know their students' needs well and to see their growth over a two-year span. They are also more able to establish effective working partnerships with students' parents. Although teachers must formally know at least a two-year curriculum, many are convinced that working this way enables them to be better teachers.

Teachers and schools contemplating alternatives to single-grade groupings will find the following section helpful.

CONSIDERING DEVELOPMENTAL STAGES IN MIXED-AGE AND MIXED-GRADE SETTINGS

My experience with mixed grouping has taught me that children of certain chronological ages are more developmentally compatible than others and thus can be grouped in the same class with better results. For example, four- and five-year-olds tend to be a difficult combination because of the completely active, outdoor, gross motor orientation of most fours and the calmer, more thoughtful demeanor of most fives. Therefore, a K–1 grouping is unlikely to work well if it has a large number of children who are still developmentally four and a large number who are solidly developmentally five or who are six.

Older fives and sixes, however, usually work well together because fives share the sixes' energetic interest in doing "real" schoolwork.

K–1 can be a good mix, therefore, when most of the kindergarten children are older fives.

Most seven-year-olds seem to thrive in a single-grade classroom. The age is characterized by a need for privacy, by sensitivity and often moodiness. If seven-year-olds must be mixed with another age, it's generally better to mix them with eights than with sixes.

Eight- and nine-year-olds (usually third and fourth graders) can generally work well together. The spread in academic abilities seems wide to many teachers, but it can be manageable if the teacher uses formats such as project work and scientific experiments, which children at both these ages love so much.

Fifth and sixth grade groupings (between ages ten and twelve) can be highly effective. Being around ten-year-olds tends to make the social struggles at school less intense for the eleven-year-olds and new twelve-year-olds. Because tens are generally more settled and school-compliant, they can have a calming influence on the older children as they make the transition into adolescence.

To meet the developmental needs of seventh and eighth graders (usually ages twelve and thirteen), mixed-age, team-taught classrooms work well. The eighth graders tend to take the seventh graders under their wing while also creating a separate space for themselves as oldest in the school (in K–8 schools especially). The seventh graders look up to the eighth graders and look forward to the privileges the next year will bring. Community service learning is a key way to link seventh and eighth graders, as children in both grades tend to find purpose in working together on projects that benefit the school or the wider community.

RETENTION

Research on retention has found that students who are retained for purely academic reasons do not benefit at all from this approach to their education and are actually seriously harmed by it. Children

The Mix of Ages in Any Single-Grade Classroom

Because of birthday differences and varying retention policies, classrooms containing a single grade level of children today will often have children of at least three different ages. (In a first-grade classroom, for example, there will often be five-, six-, and seven-year-olds; in a second grade classroom, there will be six-, seven-, and eight-year-olds.)

Appendix A, "The Birthday Cluster Exercise," describes how teachers and parents can assess and plan for the developmental "fit" of a child in a single-grade classroom in the fall and then check that fit at intervals throughout the school year.

who are retained for academic failure are much more likely to drop out of school (Nottis 2004). Yet retention rates have increased over the last twenty years. Fifteen percent of all American students are retained each year, thirty to fifty percent of them before ninth grade.

But the verb "to retain" can mean either to hold back or to keep safe. Giving young children extra time at the beginning of their school career can sometimes keep them emotionally and academically safe by giving them some extra support in these crucial early years. For retention to work in this way, we must use it only when careful screening, observation, and family consultation indicate that it will benefit the child's long-term developmental and academic growth. We must implement such supportive retention thoughtfully, through multiyear preschool and prekindergarten placements.

When we give children more time through retention, we need to monitor them carefully and provide the supports they need. For instance, children who are experiencing developmental delays due to trauma or health issues may well catch up to their peers in early learning skills if they are given proper intervention. Other children may just be developmentally younger overall and be aided simply by the extra time. The key in these considerations is high-quality early childhood screening and high-quality developmental preschool programs.

Once a child is in kindergarten, an extra year may still help ensure future success, but again, a child should not be retained for purely academic reasons. It is the job of the school to meet the academic needs of the child, not the other way around. Unfortunately, American academic grade-level standards are currently unrealistic for too many of our children. This situation creates unnecessary stress for students and schools alike. Instead of holding fast to these standards, we should focus on what we know about children's development and adjust our academic expectations for each grade accordingly. That is the proper context in which to make decisions about retention.

Cultural and Linguistic Diversity

Each child lives in a family nested in an ethnic culture or a combination of cultures. A majority of schoolchildren in America today come from a European American family culture, the same culture as most or all of the teachers they'll have during their schooling and the same culture on which their school curriculum centers. But an ever-increasing number of children in our classrooms are from African American, Latino/Hispanic, Asian American, and Native American families, or are recent immigrants from other cultures. For these children, our schools often present cultural experiences different from their home experiences. Some of the children are learning English for the first time, or learning that the response expected of them by adults in school differs from the response their parents expect at home.

Although all children in American schools share many universal aspects of child growth and development, it is important that teachers and administrators be able to see all areas of students' development through the lens of the cultural and linguistic contexts that so impact children's performance in the classroom.

CHANGES NEEDED IN AMERICAN SCHOOLS

American schools will change dramatically over the course of this century as the European American population declines and children from other cultures become the majority. In fact, according to the U.S. Department of Education (2006), this population shift is already happening in many school districts around the country. This change in population needs to be matched by changes in American schools, including diversifying the teaching profession, embracing bilingual or multilingual education, and learning about children's home cultures.

Diversifying the teaching profession

One change that would serve all children well would be a dramatic increase in the number of adults, particularly males, from non-European American backgrounds joining the elementary teaching profession. According to the U.S. Department of Education, in the 2000/2001 school year, 91 percent of the elementary teaching force was female. In the 1999/2000 school year, 82.9 percent of elementary teachers were European American, 9.6 percent African American, and 5.5 percent Latino/Hispanic. In that same year, students enrolled in public elementary schools were 61.4 percent European American, 18.1 percent African American, and 15.8 percent Latino/Hispanic

(U.S. Department of Education 2003b). Thus, at a time when an increasing percentage of students are from non-European American cultures, the percentage of teachers who are from those cultures is not keeping pace. Recruitment and retention of new teachers from nondominant cultures is one of the most difficult areas in elementary education in general. To learn about the challenges of attracting and keeping teachers of various cultural backgrounds, see *The Color of Teaching* by June A. Gordon (2000) or *Minority Teacher Recruitment, Development, and Retention* (Torres et al. 2004).

Embracing bilingual or multilingual education

Today, English is the only language most American schools choose to use or are allowed to use for instruction. This short-sighted practice must give way to an embracing of bilingual and multilingual education if we are to honor our students' cultural identities and give them the skills to live in a global economy at a time when enhanced international relations is of utmost importance.

Ten million more people in today's world speak Spanish than English, making Spanish the third most commonly spoken language worldwide, just behind Mandarin Chinese and Hindi. Increasing numbers of students in Europe, Asia, and South America already learn in bilingual and even trilingual schools and cultures. By the late twentieth century, these students represented over half the world's children (Baker and Jones 1998). American students—indeed, America itself—will benefit when national legislation and policies in this country change to embrace multiple languages as well.

Learning about children's home cultures

The cultural difference between so many of our students and their teachers means that the children often have to struggle to fit in while retaining some sense of cultural identity. Teachers can help by deepening their understanding of what each child's home culture is like and how the interaction of the home culture with American school culture may affect children's learning. They can then more effectively include and honor diverse cultures in teaching the curricula. Until educators make deliberate cultural shifts in the ways they approach teaching and learning, children from nonmainstream cultures will face major hurdles in acquiring a fair and equal education in American classrooms.

Although it will take time for large-scale cultural shifts to happen, individual teachers can begin finding ways to learn more about children's home cultures while helping children's families learn about American schools. Connecting with parents is key. Here are several ways to do that:

- Talk with parents about developmental characteristics common to all children and invite them to share ideas about important cultural differences.

- Think about how cultural differences in such things as child-rearing and discipline might affect a child's performance in school. A child used to taking direction from her mother, for example, might be confused about how to respond to a male teacher.

- Consider how cultural differences might affect school-home communication. For example, if the extended family is typically involved in child-rearing, it may be respectful to include relatives in invitations to conferences or school events.

- Help parents from all cultures feel welcome in school—for example, by sending home messages in their primary language or having an interpreter available during school and home visits.

- Invite parents to describe what they expect from their children at home, their aspirations for their child at school, something special about their child, and any concerns about their child's learning and growth.

- Welcome parents into the classroom to share aspects of their home culture with all of the children by telling a traditional story, playing a musical instrument, or using other methods they're comfortable with.

AFRICAN AMERICAN AND LATINO/HISPANIC CHILDREN

African American and Latino/Hispanic children are now the two largest minority groups in American schools. Understanding these two cultures therefore is a useful and important starting place for educators as they work to make schools richer and more productive places of learning for all children.

Although I am not an expert in educational theory as it relates to either of these two cultures, I have had direct experience with educators, parents, and students who are members of each and have studied prevailing research on issues relating to development in children from these two cultures. I hope that the brief overviews that follow and the authors I quote will lead readers to study these or similar writers in depth.

African American children

A number of researchers and scholars have helped students of child development understand that African American children face a more complex array of developmental tasks as they grow than European American children. One reason is that African American children typically live in and must learn to travel between two cultures that often have significantly different values and accepted patterns of behavior: the Black-dominated culture of their homes, neighbor-

hoods, and community entities such as religious groups; and the White-dominated culture of the wider world, which includes every-thing from school to banks to the political system (Holliday 1985, 56).

Another very important and related reason, these researchers and scholars say, is that America as a whole, to this day, still devalues African Americans. Sometimes this devaluing is subtle, but it's still enormously damaging. The fact that when we teach U.S. history, we're mostly teaching about European Americans' European her-itage and not teaching much about African Americans' African heritage is just one example of this devaluing (McAdoo 2002, 48–49; Rivers and Rivers 2002, 176; Holliday 2001, xii).

Bertha Garrett Holliday, an authority on psychological issues in eth-nic minorities, has pointed out that as a result of living bicultural lives and having to learn different roles and expectations in each cul-ture, African American children may have greater flexibility and agility in social interactions with teachers and peers. At the same time, as a result of living with racial inequality, they can be less sure whether their efforts to work hard or solve problems will in fact lead to success. They may feel undue anxiety about the unpredictability of responses from teachers and school peers. Holliday suggests that African American children tend to get "older younger," or show older social behaviors than their European American counterparts, because the unique environment they grow up in often fosters social maturity and independence (Holliday 1985, 53–69). It's important for teachers to keep that idea in mind when using this book.

Any discussion of African American children's development inevitably brings to mind the question of these children's school achievement and the disturbing fact that in most standardized measures of school achievement, they score lower on the whole than European American students. Just as disturbing is the all too common belief among educators and the public that the reason for this lower achievement is that African American children come to school lagging behind European American peers in developmental abilities or lacking the skills necessary for school success. Holliday's research throws doubt on this belief. Other researchers, too, have convincingly countered this idea that African American homes or communities have some sort of deficit when it comes to raising their children for success. The highly respected sociology professor Harriette Pipes McAdoo, for example, points to the extended family support system and the deep church involvement of many African American families as strengths that help the children deal with adversities (McAdoo 2002, 49; McAdoo 2007, 99).

Janice Hale-Benson, who has written widely on the education of African American children, emphasizes that lower achievement among African American children is often a function of the way they are perceived and treated by their teachers, rather than a function of their home or community culture. Many researchers, she notes, have found that teachers expect more from European American students than from African American students. In general, she writes, teachers expect the most from European American females, followed by European American males, then African American females, and finally African American males (Hale-Benson 2001, 1982). Of course it is seldom the intent of any teacher to expect less from some students than others, and increased professional development in cross-cultural interactions will help teachers recognize the strengths in our African American students and avoid unintentionally lowering our expectations concerning their ability to succeed in school.

In her most recent work, Hale-Benson presents a strong model for helping African American children do well in school. That can be done, she says, by connecting African American students, especially boys, to academic achievement at an early age. Hale-Benson calls on school principals to be accountable to the community for this achievement (Hale-Benson 2001, xvii, xxiv).

I agree with Hale-Benson's call. As school leaders, principals have a special mandate to be clear with teachers and parents alike that the entire school community is responsible for the progress of every child. Further, principals must ensure that every parent feels comfortable making an appointment to talk directly with them, as well as with their child's teacher. This, truly, would help us achieve "no child left behind."

Latino/Hispanic children

When it comes to Latino/Hispanic children's development, one of the most contentious and misunderstood areas is their language and literacy development. Many Latino/Hispanic children use Spanish at home, and there is great debate among educators over whether to use both English and Spanish when teaching them in school and, if using both, exactly how to do it.

Much of the controversy appears to stem from persistent myths concerning bilingualism. Gloria G. Rodriguez, early childhood educator and founder of Avance, a Latino/Hispanic parent support and education organization, notes that "society is filled with exaggerated and negative ideas about bilingualism." Here are four "beliefs" that Rodriguez (1999, 148–9) characterizes as myths: Bilingualism is harmful to children since they cannot learn either language well; being bilingual can result in prolonged and permanent delays in language development; bilingualism confuses children; and children must speak English only or they will not be accepted in mainstream society.

Contrary to these myths, we know through research the following to be true:

- Bilingual children can learn both languages well.

- Being bilingual does not permanently delay language development.

- Bilingualism does not confuse children.

- Bilingual ability is increasingly being valued by mainstream society, including top U.S. corporations and the U.S. government.

(Reyes and Moll 2005)

Writing to the Latino/Hispanic community, Rodriguez says:

> You should remind your child, as he grows older, that a person who is multilingual will be able to communicate with more people and be understood in different settings.... When our young children become adults, they will comprise the largest ethnic group in our country. Therefore, if they are to become leaders, they will have to know Spanish in order to relate to and understand a greater number of people. Knowledge is power, and the persons who understand and are able to communicate with more people will have the power. (Rodriguez 1999, 147)

Work by University of Arizona researchers Iliana Reyes and Luis Moll on Mexican American children, a large segment of the Latino/Hispanic population, further sheds light on the debate. Their research looks at how children learn languages, something that anyone who teaches children from Spanish-speaking homes should understand in order to teach these children well. First we must make a distinction between bilingualism (the ability to speak two languages) and biliteracy (the ability to read and write in two languages). Reyes and Moll note that studies suggest it takes approximately two years to become orally proficient in a second language (bilingual) and about five to seven years to reach an average native speaker's level of reading and writing performance (biliterate) (Reyes and Moll 2005, 6).

This means that a child from a Spanish-speaking home who enters an English-speaking school might converse in English within two years, but may not be able to read, write, and take tests in English at grade level for five to seven years. Many children, in their first years of learning English, do poorly in English-speaking classes and on tests written in English. Reyes and Moll say this is not a sign that they are incapable of being bilingual or biliterate. The problem, rather, is that schools are rushing them into performing in English before they can reasonably be expected to do so. To then limit these children to learning in English in hopes of speeding their English acquisition will do more harm than good and in fact could rob them of the enormous gift of bilingualism and biliteracy.

Another common misperception related to Latino/Hispanic children's literacy development is that these children receive no support outside school for developing literacy skills in any language. On the contrary, Reyes and colleagues, in studying Mexican American families with preschoolers, have found that many of these parents are constantly teaching their children early literacy skills at home—in both Spanish and English. They do so through such activities as making shopping lists in English and Spanish and role playing in both languages (Reyes, Alexandra, and Azuava 2006). Here are other findings from Reyes's research:

- Mothers in the households studied often provide rich literacy events such as storytelling, role playing, singing and dancing, playing with puppets, and showing their children how to participate in cultural traditional activities (for example, making flour tortillas, tamales, a piñata). These events and activities are usually related to their home country's arts, crafts, music, and literary heritage and help their children become biliterate preschoolers.

- Teachers and educators often do not recognize these as literacy-teaching practices because they may not match those used by European American middle-class families. For example, European American middle-class families tend to read books with or to their children, whereas the Mexican American families might tell a family legend, asking the child to change the ending.

- English plays a predominant role in print material shared with the children at home in the families studied.

- Given that children are instructed primarily in English at school, the use of Spanish during literacy events at home is a way of enabling children to become biliterate.

(Reyes 2006; Reyes, Alexandra, and Azuara 2006)

We can conclude from Reyes's and colleagues' work that if children from Spanish-speaking homes are given enough opportunities to function in Spanish as well as English, they will continue to develop their bilingualism and potentially their biliteracy. It's important, therefore, for teachers to learn about how Spanish-speaking parents' home literacy practices impact the children's overall biliteracy learning, value such home efforts, and work to bring home and school teaching in concert with each other.

Yardsticks: Broad Guidelines

The "yardsticks," or guidelines, in this section are designed to help teachers and parents understand how developmental milestones may affect the way children at different ages and in different grades experience school. As you will see in the charts that follow, I have sorted the developmental information for each age into three categories:

- *Growth Patterns:* This category covers developmental milestones and common patterns in children's physical, social-emotional, language, and cognitive growth.

- *In the Classroom:* This category lists ways that children's typical abilities in the physical, cognitive (including language), and social-emotional realms at each age shape how they naturally work and play in school.

- *Curriculum:* This category constitutes a "subject-at-a-glance" look at how I believe curriculum expectations should take into account children's developmental stages. These pages offer detailed suggestions for age-appropriate tasks and materials in reading, writing, and mathematics. Also included are ideas for thematic units that can span social studies, current events, and science.

A Word about the Curriculum Category

The information in the curriculum charts may surprise some readers, based as it is on the developmental needs of children rather than the strict educational content standards set by policymakers and test designers today. For instance, these days schools expect children much younger than ten to be adept at content memorization in math, vocabulary, and grammar. The curriculum guidelines here, however, suggest asking children to do extensive memorizing only when they reach ten, the age at which their skills at this activity are usually at their zenith.

As suggested by such differences from typical content standards, these yardsticks reflect my deep belief in the need for a developmentally based curriculum, especially now, when we again find ourselves in a highly charged, standards-based educational climate, not unlike the "back to basics" movement in the early 1970s. This educational climate drives the lockstep rushing of children through a state-mandated curriculum that's a mile wide and an inch deep.

The developmental approach I advocate in this book, on the other hand, argues for depth over breadth, and for adapting curriculum to fit children's emotional, social, cognitive, language, and physical needs. Certainly, academic learning is important. But while exercising vigilant oversight of children's developing skills in math and reading, we must remember that academic achievement is not the only important part of school. Furthermore, academic skill development is honed and enhanced by its application to other areas of learning. It's also important that children come to love learning, creativity, and problem solving for their own sake.

Parents can help make sure this happens by reviewing the curriculum charts in this book as their children grow to see what sorts of school experiences are appropriate for them. Parents can then check in at school to see what kinds of experiences their children's teachers are providing. For example, are the children being offered

homework choices, not just homework "have to's"? Are they participating in hands-on learning experiences such as science experiments, field trips, and learning fairs or exhibitions? Along with math workbook pages, do children bring home math surveys that encourage them to observe, count, and measure objects in their environment?

As children move into the intermediate grades, nurturing their growth as eager learners means paying special attention to the regularity of their independent reading. Too many children in the third grade and up insist that they don't have to read, hate reading, or finished all their reading in school. Neither television nor the Internet can replace the depth of learning experienced in a half-hour of independent reading, without interruption, at home every night.

As you explore the curriculum charts, please remember that chronological age and cognitive growth do not necessarily go hand in hand. Some children, for instance, will be ready for reading instruction at an early age, whereas others may not be ready to read until after the "expected" age. Schools are often too quick to label the latter children learning disabled or remedial. On the other hand, waiting too long for reading to emerge (past first grade) before intervening can also be hurtful. Most schools now do diagnostic work at the beginning, middle, and end of kindergarten and first grade. A similar diagnostic screening is now used by most schools to better understand student ability to tackle basic mathematical concepts such as simple counting, measurement, beginning addition and subtraction, and basic algebraic thinking and problem solving.

Included in the "Writing" section of each set of curriculum charts you'll find information about typical writing, spelling, and handwriting abilities as well as children's age-related interests. Again, remember that development in these areas does not always correspond neatly to a specific chronological age. Writing, spelling, and topical interests are tied to children's cognitive development and to their home cultures; handwriting is related to both cognitive and physical development.

In the "Thematic Units" section, I offer favorite topics or focus areas for children at each age. Thematic teaching allows classroom teachers to weave a wide range of subject matter and varied enrichments (such as art and music) into the elementary curriculum. Teachers can use reading and language arts instruction to help the children learn social studies, science, and math at their own academic level and through content they find exciting.

When teaching thematically, today's teachers must work together across grade levels to create a continuum of curriculum that meets state standards while addressing age-appropriate developmental needs. This type of teaching is compatible with offering choices of assignments that are differentiated to meet the needs of all students—a teaching approach that is increasingly accepted nationwide, if not always possible to implement fully.

Using the Yardsticks Charts

Teachers can use the yardsticks charts to help understand each child and each year's group of children as they lead students along the path of learning. As a result of what they learn from the yardsticks, teachers may reconsider how to group students for seat work or activities. Or perhaps thinking about the developmental themes significant for children at a particular age will give teachers fresh ideas about the read-aloud books likely to grab student interest.

(See Appendix D, "Some Favorite Books for Children at Different Ages," as well as the charts.) Experienced teachers can check and compare these yardsticks with their own understanding of children based on their years in the classroom, and new teachers will find it interesting to compare their university learning in child development with these benchmarks.

Parents can use these yardsticks to evaluate how curriculum and classroom life seem to fit the needs of the child they know so well. The yardsticks can also help parents understand their son's or daughter's behavior at home. If you're a parent, just reading about the common characteristics of a certain age often provides helpful reminders about how to look lovingly at behavior that may be driving you crazy right now. "I realized it was not just my child acting like this," I've heard more than one parent remark with relief.

Whether you are a teacher or parent, please remember that these milestones are based largely on research about children from European American cultural backgrounds. How child development patterns are expressed will differ from culture to culture. Therefore, it's important for all of us to learn more about the specific developmental expressions in various cultures, perhaps starting with some of the references listed in this book.

Finally, please keep firmly in mind as you use the following charts that personality plays a clear and often dramatic role in the way children move through developmental stages. Shy and quiet children will move through their childhood one way, loud and active children another. Many people believe gender plays a role in development (boys are usually thought to mature more slowly in most areas through adolescence), and researchers are interested in how boys and girls differ in their approach to such issues as friendship, social problem solving, and math and science learning.

The most important lesson to take away here is that each child is an individual: His or her development will be unique even though it fits within a broad developmental pattern. With that truth in mind, the yardsticks in this book are offered not as standards for children to live up to, but as general indicators to help guide teachers and parents in understanding children's growth.

All the world's a stage
And all the men and women merely players:
They have their exits and their entrances;
And one man in his time plays many parts
His acts being seven ages. At the first the infant,
Mewling and puking in the nurse's arms.
And then the whining school-boy, with his satchel
And shining morning face, creeping like snail
Unwilling to school.

WILLIAM SHAKESPEARE, *AS YOU LIKE IT*, ACT II, SCENE VI

Four-Year-Olds

"Give me my Bunny!" he said.
"You mustn't say that. He isn't a toy. He's REAL!"

The Velveteen Rabbit | *by Margery Williams*

When my son was four years old, we lived on a paved country road that saw occasional but speedy traffic. One Saturday morning, a worried motorist knocked on the door. "Do you have a little boy and a dog? If you do, they're a half mile up the road and moving fast." The yard gate had been opened by intelligent fingers for the first time and boy and dog had made their escape into the world. Fortunately, we retrieved them safely, changed the gate lock, and continued our education of, and by, the four-year-old. Our story could have had a different ending: The news occasionally delivers tragic stories of parents losing adventurous young children between parked cars, out open windows, or off fire escapes.

Fours tend to be ready for everything. They are explorers and adventurers who are soaking up the world of knowledge with incredible speed. They are capable of almost nonstop mental and physical gymnastics. Children at four love to exaggerate. A four-year-old's tall tale about a villain who followed him home from school may worry a parent or teacher, but not the four-year-old.

Parents and teachers need vast amounts of energy to keep up with these young dynamos.

Four-year-olds are present in our public school classrooms, not just in prekindergarten and Head Start. Many school districts admit children who turn five by December 31 of a given school year. Thus, many children are still four when they enter kindergarten (and still three when they begin a prekindergarten or Head Start program). Children at four demand school programs that are flexible, exciting, and creative because these children are flexible, exciting, and creative creatures. They respond joyfully to dance, creative movement, outdoor play, and drama.

Short attention spans match four-year-olds' short bodies. Head Start, prekindergarten, and kindergarten programs must reflect this tendency to switch quickly from one interest to another. Activity centers (or areas of the room) should be arranged so fours can move from center to center or area to area across the room without a lot of traffic congestion. Visually, four-year-olds tend to look toward the horizon, so room setups that provide plenty of space for children's movements minimize accidents and knock-overs.

Preschool and kindergarten teachers should minimize paper and pencil tasks for four-year-olds. Fours learn best through their own play, by being read to, by acting out stories and fairy tales, and by manipulating clay, paintbrushes, finger paints, building blocks, and math materials. Outdoor play is also essential for fours; they should spend at least a quarter of their school day in physical activity. This is an age when much learning is transmitted through the large muscles, when learning goes from the hand to the head, not the other way around. Those teaching four-year-olds need to focus on observing the children, reinforcing their appropriate behavior, reminding or redirecting them when their behavior begins to go off track, and asking them questions that lead them toward the next level of cognitive exploration and understanding.

Four-Year-Olds: Growth Patterns

PHYSICAL

- Tend to focus visually on faraway objects

- Often clumsy; collisions and spills are common

- Because fine motor skills are not well developed, they typically grasp pencil in whole fist and use their arm, hand, and fingers as a single unit; young fours may hold pencil more tentatively toward the eraser and write with a very light stroke; older fours write more boldly and firmly

- Need lots of physical activity—running, jumping, climbing, and dancing

- Able to sit still only for short periods

SOCIAL-EMOTIONAL

- Friendly, talkative, "bubbly"

- Love being with friends, though they still often work near, not with, a friend

- Not overly dependent on adults and can make decisions based on their own interests, but need adult advice

- Need adult help finding words to express needs, instead of reacting physically

- Love "jobs" such as taking attendance or putting out snack at school and setting the table or folding clothes at home

- Older fours are sometimes fearful or worried and may have nightmares

- *Very* talkative; enjoy experimenting with language, delighting in big words, long explanations, bathroom language, and swear words

- Love being read to

LANGUAGE

- Have short attention spans; move quickly from one thing to the next

- Learn best by moving large muscles

- Need to play and explore; love dress-up and drama

- Enjoy activities that use music, rhythm, repeating patterns, and other simple learning strategies

COGNITIVE

Four-Year-Olds in the Classroom

VISION AND **FINE MOTOR ABILITY**	■ Not ready for close visual activity (such as reading or writing); should do very little paper and pencil work that focuses only on mechanical skills; instead, they can boost their early literacy skills by scribbling and using invented spelling ■ Unable to switch smoothly between near and far focus; should never be asked to copy from the board ■ Use their whole hand to write; printing is usually large
GROSS MOTOR ABILITY	■ Awkward with writing, handcrafts, and other small movements; learn more through large muscle activity and play, such as hauling large blocks, than through paper-and-pencil activities ■ Need climbing apparatus on the playground ■ In physical education class, usually enjoy tumbling ■ Ready for pre-writing; finger painting or painting with brushes at stand-up easels gives them excellent practice
COGNITIVE GROWTH	■ Love being read to—whether individually, in small groups, or as whole class; love to do their own "reading" of picture books ■ Constantly reading their environment—labeling objects that children frequently see or use gives them many opportunities to practice *continued on next page*

- Need many hands-on experiences; all classroom areas should have manipulatives such as magnets, pulleys, puzzles, interlocking cubes, scoops, funnels, measuring cups, and sand

- Ready to practice counting through "real" jobs such as taking attendance and doing the milk count

- Move quickly from one thing to another; hard for them to stay in one area of the classroom for an extended time

- Can learn responsibilities that are carefully taught (for example, room cleanup at the end of a work period), but need the teacher to model expectations

- Learn from modeling; need chances to practice new behavior

- Easily redirected from inappropriate behavior; teacher language is very important in helping children use language instead of physical means: "Use words," "Tell her what you want," "Ask if he is finished," etc.; small dramas and role plays help teach social skills

- Love learning to work together, although playing next to (instead of with) other children may continue for younger fours; "Who's the boss?" is often the major developmental issue; can learn basic mediation skills, but the teacher's saying "It's the rule" works wonders

- Tend to roughhouse on the playground; need teacher redirection and modeling of appropriate behavior; for example, to a youngster rushing for the stairs, say "Jessie, stop!", followed (once the child has complied) by "Now go down the stairs safely—watch how I do it; then you try"

Four-Year-Olds: Curriculum

Provide opportunities for children this age to:

- Be read to, especially from picture books with repetitive words

- Be storytellers as well as listeners

- Build the sequences of reading by using predictable books—those with repeating phrases and few words, or pictures and no words

- Do "parallel" reading with an adult: The child "reads" one page of a familiar book (tells the story while looking at the words and pictures), and the adult reads the next

WRITING

Expect from these children:

- *Beginning Spelling:* Prephonemic—many letters do not correspond to sounds; for example, they will write or say "B-H-K-E-E-E-E-E-E-E-J-B" for sailboat

- *Writing Themes:* Fascination with blood and gore, fantasy, TV takeoffs, fairy tales, and pets

- *Handwriting:* Mainly scribble writing and drawing

THEMATIC UNITS

(Social Studies, Science, Current Events)

Favorite themes for children this age:

- Dinosaurs

- All about me

- Transportation (cars, trucks, trains, and planes)

- Houses

Provide opportunities for children this age to:

- Explore size, shape, length, and volume through manipulating solid blocks, large interlocking cubes, sand, and water

- Count and sort objects

- Explore math through stories

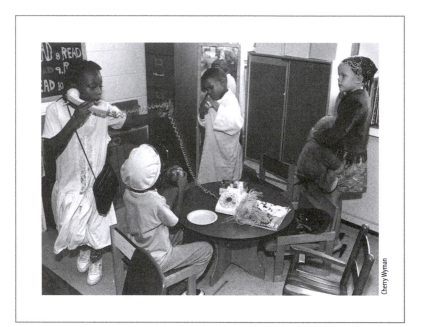

Five-Year-Olds

"Ramona loved Miss Binney so much she did not want to disappoint her. Not ever. Miss Binney was the nicest teacher in the whole world."

Ramona the Pest | *by Beverly Cleary*

After a busy morning in an overly academic kindergarten, a five-year-old boy marched up to his teacher's desk, put his hands on his hips, and announced, "You don't seem to understand, teacher; I just came here to eat and play!" Nothing could better characterize the developmental needs of the five-year-old than this story from my colleague, Sue Sweitzer.

Today, many of our kindergarten and first grade programs are once more seriously out of balance with the developmental needs of five-year-olds. Too much attention to paper and pencil tasks, test taking, and early reading acquisition is creating a pressure cooker environment for children, teachers, and parents.

Learning is at its best for five-year-olds when it is both structured and exploratory: structured through a clear and predictable schedule; exploratory through carefully constructed interest areas where children can initiate their own activity. The best teachers observe children's learning activities and then create teacher-directed instruction to complement the children's interests and meet the learning expectations for the age.

Five, overall, is a time of great happiness. Life is "good," says the five-year-old. A primary objective in life seems to be pleasing significant adults. Fives are constantly asking, "Mom, can I set the table? Can I put away the socks?" At school, five-year-olds also ask permission: "Teacher, can I use these markers? Teacher, is this how you do it? How much can I use, teacher?"

Five-year-olds need permission from adults to make transitions, to move from task to task. Fives are literal and usually accept adult rules as absolute and unbendable. In *Ramona the Pest* (Cleary 1968), Ramona wouldn't budge from her seat the first day in kindergarten because her teacher, Miss Binney, had told her to "sit here for the present." Certain that she needed to do exactly as her teacher said— and misunderstanding Miss Binney's use of the word "present"— Ramona was sure if she stayed in her seat, Miss Binney would give her some sort of wonderful gift.

Although many children have by now been in social settings with peers outside the home for several years, kindergarten remains a time of immense social interest. Children love to explore the world of "real school" together. Fantasy play, dress-up, housekeeping, and play with puppets continue to be essential for growth and development. Sadly, many of these essential learning activities have been dropped from kindergarten programs.

Five-year-olds are not selfish, but they are at the center of their own universe and often find it hard to see the world from any other point of view. Children may find it impossible to complete a given task except in the one way they know—their way. They often have trouble expressing empathy if a conflict affects them directly— sharing their toys or space, for example—but if a classmate across the room is crying, a crowd of caring fives may gather.

Young five-year-olds seem in a period of consolidation, resting from the exuberant, somewhat wild behavior of four. At four children exaggerate, tell long stories, talk constantly, and are always in motion. At five, they are a little calmer, more literal and exact.

One-word answers—"good" and "fine"—replace elaborate explanations. Parents who try to get answers to the question, "What did you
do in school today?" may find fives frustrating.

At five, children's vision most easily focuses on objects near to them.
They become engrossed in the details of a block construction or a
complicated painting. Because they cannot easily sweep their eyes
laterally across a printed page, left-to-right and right-to-left, most
five-year-olds are not ready for formal reading instruction.

It is especially important to remember that five-year-olds do not
think the same way about the world as adults do. Cause and effect
are not explained through logic, but rather through intuition. Five-
year-old thought that appears illogical—for example, "I go to sleep
because it's night"—can be considered pre-logical. Bound by the
senses, restricted to what they can see, fives must act on one thing
at a time. The best kindergarten teachers know that they, too, must
focus on one thing at a time, keeping expectations clear and simple.

Children generally move through two distinct developmental phases during the kindergarten year—one of caution, literalness, and general compliance; a second of experimentation, oppositional behavior, and uncertainty. Some aspects of these developmental phases result from visual and perceptual changes (as in letter and number reversals). Others are related to changing cognitive patterns as children move from pre-operational learning, bounded by the senses, to new and more complex, yet still concrete, thinking patterns. Like other changes, this shift in thinking patterns creates tension and disequilibrium.

As five-year-olds move toward six, visual and auditory confusions commonly show up in reversals of letters and numbers. The child is not sure which way things go and says so. "Maybe" replaces "Yes!" An emphatic "NO" may remind us of the "terrible two's." Children are testing the limits they were so comfortable with a few months ago. Earlier in the year, sitting still and listening was easier. Now there are wiggles and complaints and it's not uncommon to see children falling sideways out of their chairs. (At six, they often fall over backwards.)

As children move toward six, their language becomes more differentiated and complex. They like to explain things and to have things explained to them. Their behavior also becomes more complex. Children can play well one moment and argue the next. They may delight in independent activity or become instantly dependent on adult intervention. Sometimes they dawdle, sometimes they rush. Initiative drives them forward. The more they can do on their own, the stronger they feel. But they also hate to fail at tasks. With the support of sympathetic adults, however, five-year-olds will keep trying, and their efforts will engender feelings of self-worth and purposefulness. This prepares children to venture into a lengthy period of industrious learning between the ages of six and eleven.

Five-Year-Olds: Growth Patterns

PHYSICAL	■ Focus visually on objects close at hand
	■ Need lots of physical activity, including free play
	■ Better control of running, jumping, and other large movements; still awkward with writing, handcrafts, and other small movements
	■ Pace themselves well, resting before they're exhausted
	■ Hold pencils with three-fingered, pincer-like grasp
	■ Often fall out of chairs sideways
SOCIAL-EMOTIONAL	■ Like to help, cooperate, follow rules, and be "good"; want adult approval
	■ Need routines, along with consistent rules and discipline; respond well to clear and simple expectations
	■ Dependent on authority, but also have trouble seeing things from another's viewpoint
	■ Need verbal permission from adults; before doing something, will ask, "Can I . . . ?"

- Literal, using and interpreting words in their usual or most basic sense: "We're late—we've got to fly!" means "We've got to take to the air like birds!"

- Express themselves in few words; "play" and "good" are favorites

- Often do not talk about school happenings at home

- Express fantasy more through actions and less through words than at four

- Think out loud—that is, they talk their thoughts

- Like to copy and repeat activities

- Often see only one way to do things

- Bound cognitively by their senses; not ready to understand abstract concepts such as "fairness"

- Ascribe life and movement to inanimate objects such as stuffed animals

- Learn best through active play and hands-on activities

- Think intuitively rather than logically; for example, "It's windy when the trees shake, so it must be the shaking of the trees that makes the wind"

Five-Year-Olds in the Classroom

VISION AND FINE MOTOR ABILITY	- Still developing left-to-right visual tracking, so they tend to focus on one word at a time when reading; often need to use a pointer or their finger to keep their place - Still have difficulty copying from the board - Occasionally reverse letters and numbers (either swapping positions, as in writing "ot" for "to," or drawing the letters themselves backwards so that a "d," for example, looks like a "b"); teachers can help by accepting these reversals without comment, rather than correcting - Ready for an introduction to manuscript printing; not able to stay within lines - Find it hard to space letters, numbers, and words; using a finger as a separator helps
GROSS MOTOR ABILITY	- As at four, continue to need a great deal of active outdoor and indoor physical activity - Enjoy structured games such as Duck, Duck, Goose and Red Light, Green Light

- Learn best through repetition; like to repeat stories, poems, songs, and games, sometimes with minor variations; enjoy sets of similar math and science tasks; need predictable daily schedules

- Some become stuck in repetitive behavior (for example, always drawing rainbows or flowers) for fear of making mistakes when trying something new

- Learn best through active exploration of materials such as blocks, manipulatives, clay, sand, and water

- Seldom able to see things from another's point of view

- Think out loud; will say, for example, "I'm going to move the truck!" before doing so

- Can work at quiet, sitting activities for fifteen to twenty minutes at a time

- Often need their teacher's release to move to the next task, though they can pace themselves while doing a given task

- Feel safe with consistent guidelines and carefully planned periods

- Express thoughts through action; need opportunities to play in housekeeping or other dramatic play corners

- Learn and practice language skills through teacher modeling and directed role play, as well as dramatic play

Older Five-Year-Olds: Growth Patterns

PHYSICAL

- Tend to be physically restless and to tire quickly

- Awkwardly perform tasks requiring fine motor skills

- Vary their pencil grasp

- Tilt their head to their nondominant side when writing

- Complain that their hand gets tired from holding their pencil

- Often stand up to work

- Oppositional; not sure whether to be good or naughty

- Insecure with feelings and tentative in actions

- Complain, test authority and limits, and strike out with temper tantrums

- Behave wonderfully at home and terribly at school, or vice versa

- Equivocate, switching answers from "yes" to "no" and vice versa

LANGUAGE

- Begin giving more elaborate answers to questions

- Tend to use more words than necessary to convey an idea

- Frequently make auditory reversals (answer first what they heard last)

- Often read out loud even when asked to read silently

COGNITIVE

- Begin to try new activities more easily

- Make lots of mistake and recognize some of them

- Learn well from direct experience

Older Five-Year-Olds in the Classroom

VISION AND FINE MOTOR ABILITY	■ Print less neatly and with more reversals than earlier in the year ■ Grasp pencil very firmly; placing pencil grips on their pencils encourages relaxation ■ Reverse letters and numbers with increasing frequency; may find reading and writing activities extremely frustrating if not closely related to their interests
GROSS MOTOR ABILITY	■ Need a good deal of physical activity and relaxed, free play outside because attention is not always focused in a structured gym class ■ Tire quickly; sometimes need shorter work periods than younger fives
COGNITIVE GROWTH	■ Still use language to initiate action ("I'm going to pet the dog"); begin to explain in more detail ■ Need many avenues—building with blocks, painting, working with clay—to express what they know ■ Need time to try their own ways of doing things, even though these ways may not prove productive ■ Crave constant validation of their initiative

- Need consistent rules and discipline even more than earlier in the year

- Because children are testing limits more, harsh discipline (especially for mistakes) can be devastating; they respond better to frequent reminders and redirection ("Jimmy, what do you need to do to clean up?" "Lisa, hands in your lap.")

Five-Year-Olds: Curriculum

Provide opportunities for children this age to:

- Do "partner" reading—peers helping each other through familiar books; more able readers may pair well with more beginning readers, but both need to play an active role (as in "parallel" reading)

- Have short chapter books read to them

- Write theme stories with classmates and turn them into books

- Strengthen their reading skills by reading predictable books (books with few words, much repetition, and many pictures)

- Learn phonics in small groups with children at similar skill levels

- Read labels, signs, posters, and charts identifying familiar objects in their environment

Expect from these children:

- *Writing:* Labeling of drawings with initial consonants or vowels to stand for one feature in the drawing (as in "H" for "house" in a drawing of houses, people, and trees); tell stories in a single drawing and one or two words

- *Beginning Spelling:* Largely prephonemic or early phonemic—beginning to use initial consonants or vowels to represent words and sometimes stringing

continued on next page

those initial letters together in "sentences" such as I STBFL (I see the butterfly)

- *Writing Themes:* Family, family trips, fairy tales, tales of good and evil, stories about pets, and stories about themselves and best friends

- *Handwriting:* Switch to three-fingered pencil grasp; tendency to write only uppercase letters; as understanding of spelling develops, use of irregular spacing between words

Favorite themes for children this age:

- Families
- All about me
- My body
- Babies
- Pets
- Our school
- Seasonal themes in nature (snow, winter, hibernation)

Provide opportunities for children this age to:

- Count and sort, make sets, do simple addition and subtraction using real materials, and make graphs

- Practice writing numbers

- Do simple equations

- Continue hands-on exploration of size, shape, length, and volume

Six-Year-Olds

"But now I am six, I'm clever as clever.
So I think I'll be six for ever and ever."

Now We Are Six | *by A. A. Milne*

One of my favorite children's books about school is *First Grade Takes a Test* by Miriam Cohen (1980/2006). In this book, the children are confounded by the experience of taking a timed test for the first time. They have to keep still, answer questions without help from their friends, and finish within a specified period of time. Several hilarious examples of six-year-old thinking show that sixes are not at all ready for formal testing. Here's my favorite:

> *On the test there was a picture of Sally and Tom. Sally was giving Tom something. It looked like a bologna sandwich. Underneath it said:*
>
> ☐ *Sally is taller than Tom.*
> ☐ *Tom is taller than Sally.*
>
> *Jim wondered what being tall had to do with getting a bologna sandwich. And was it really a bologna sandwich? It might be tomato . . . Jim took a long time on that one.*

In today's educational environment, six-year-olds are often asked to master tests much more complicated than this. Understanding of young children's needs in the classroom seems lacking in today's standards-driven educational climate.

Six is an age of dramatic physical, cognitive, and social change. Tooth eruption is continuous; first grade teachers find chewed pencils, papers, and workbook corners in the first grade. Visual development is maturing, allowing for easy introduction of beginning reading tasks. Rapid physical growth is mirrored in rapid physical activity. Children are constantly in a hurry, rushing to be finished. They love to do their assignments, but are decidedly more interested in the process than in the product. Schoolwork tends to be sloppy or variable in quality. Children show great interest in being first, in doing the most work, or in the opposite extreme: Those who can't be first may gladly be last; dawdling can be a favorite pastime. Along with great bursts of energy come periods of fatigue and frequent illnesses.

"Industrious" describes the overall behavior of children at six. Classrooms full of six-year-olds are busy, noisy places. Talking, humming, whistling, and bustling are the order of the day. The children are now as interested in schoolwork as in spontaneous play. The importance of friends now rivals the importance of parents and teachers in the child's social development, and children delight in cooperative projects, activities, and tasks. No job is too big, no mountain too high. Their enthusiasms, however, can outstrip their skills, and sixes risk an overpowering sense of inadequacy and inferiority as they tackle new frontiers. Teachers and parents need to remember that at this age, the process is more important than the product.

As the six-year-old works hard to order and structure the world in new ways, an ounce of encouragement produces a radiant smile, hugs, and excitement. An ounce of condemnation can produce tears, pouting, and withdrawal. A teacher's words, tone, and body language all have a great effect on six-year-olds.

It is at six that most children begin a major transition in their intellectual growth. When they are younger, children are unable to accommodate an adult view of reality and generally don't understand adult explanations of cause and effect (although they may accept such explanations without challenge). Now learning to approach the world more logically, children begin to organize concepts symbolically and systematically.

The beginning of reasoning is marked by the child's ability to identify differences, compensate for these differences, and reverse an idea through mental activity. In one classic example of child psychologist Jean Piaget's, a six-year-old will see two equal balls of clay as equal quantities even after one is rolled out into a clay "snake" and compared with the ball. Younger children, able to hold onto only one idea at a time, will see the "snake" as containing more clay because it is longer.

Most six-year-olds begin to show a shift in reasoning, an understanding of cause and effect in the natural world (for example, what makes the clouds move), and a widening vision. Sixes can begin to see another's point of view and consider rules and conduct with greater objectivity.

In many ways this is a key moment, a turning point, an open door. At six, the child is extremely receptive to all new learning. The eagerness, curiosity, imagination, drive, and enthusiasm of the six-year-old are perhaps never again matched in quantity or intensity during the life span.

Cherry Wyman

Six-Year-Olds: Growth Patterns

PHYSICAL

- Good visual tracking from left to right

- More aware of their fingers as tools

- Noisy and sloppy; in a hurry; speed is a hallmark of six

- Often fall backwards out of their chairs

- Learning to distinguish left from right

- Because they're teething, they often chew on pencils, fingernails, hair, books, and other objects

- Tire easily; frequently ill

- Enjoy being active both outdoors and in the gym

SOCIAL-EMOTIONAL

- Want to be first

- Competitive; enthusiastic

- Sometimes "poor sports" or dishonest; invent rules to enable themselves to win

- Anxious to do well

- Thrive on encouragement

- Tremendous capacity for enjoyment; like surprises and treats

- Can be bossy, teasing, or critical of others

- Easily upset when hurt

continued on next page

- Care a great deal about friends; may have a best friend

- Less influenced by happenings at home than at school

- Enjoy explaining things; sharing about things they like helps develop their language skills

- Use boisterous and enthusiastic language

- Love jokes and guessing games

- Tend to complain frequently

- Learn best through discovery; love asking questions and trying out new games and ideas

- Better understand spatial and functional relationships

- Very ambitious and motivated to learn; may choose projects that are too hard

- Enjoy the process more than the product

- Love to color and paint

- Engage in more elaborate cooperative and dramatic play than at five

- Increasingly interested in computers

- Beginning to understand past and present and also how and why things happen

- Beginning to be interested in skill and technique for their own sake

- Like to "work"; enjoy reading and writing

Six-Year-Olds in the Classroom

VISION AND FINE MOTOR ABILITY	■ Will copy from the board, but find it very difficult; some schools use personalized whiteboards ■ When writing, find spacing and staying on the line difficult ■ Ability to track visually from left to right readies them for reading instruction
GROSS MOTOR ABILITY	■ Comfortable with a busy level of noise and activity; often work standing ■ Can produce products of higher quality when encouraged to work more slowly or when teachers limit the number or complexity of tasks
COGNITIVE GROWTH	■ Enjoy and learn from games of all sorts; poems, riddles, and songs delight them and teach more effectively than workbooks ■ Experience an artistic explosion; children seriously experiment with clay, paints, dancing, coloring, book making, weaving, and singing; need to feel that their attempts are valued, that there is no right and wrong way to approach art; risk-taking now enhances later artistic expression and competence

continued on next page

- Proudly produce a great quantity of work but are unconcerned with quality; whatever the activity—whether academics, cleanup, or snack—their delight lies in the doing (especially when doing for themselves)

- Need social studies content connected to here and now; find history difficult unless it is closely associated with the present

- Enjoy and learn much from field trips followed by representational activities such as telling about the trips or using blocks to recreate things they saw

- Use tantrums, teasing, bossing, complaining, and tattling to try out relationships with authority; learn best when adults understand but do not excessively tolerate this behavior

- Extremely sensitive—an ounce of encouragement may be all they need to get through a difficult situation; severe criticism can truly injure them

- Highly competitive, can overdo the need to win and be first; do better when teachers take the competitive edge off games used for learning

- Ready to try taking on individual and group responsibility

Six-Year-Olds: Curriculum

READING

Provide opportunities for children this age to:

- Continue to do partner reading

- Continue phonics learning by doing guided reading with the whole class and in small groups

- Continue reading predictable books while beginning to move on to easy chapter books

- Use writing, drawing, clay, painting, drama, or blocks to show their thoughts and feelings about a story

- Show their understanding of differences between genres (for example, poetry versus essay)

WRITING

Expect from these children:

- *Writing:* Story development still strongly influenced by drawings—for example, stories may be based on a collection of drawings; ability to write whole sentences, even if these sentences are early phonemic or use "letter name" spelling strategies—"I WNT TO HR HS" for "I went to her house"

- *Beginning Spelling:* Letter naming and "transitional" spelling (My frends ride bickes); emerging sense of phonetic clues

- *Writing Themes:* Best friends, school-related stories, family, pets, going on trips, new possessions, holidays, fantasy

- *Handwriting:* Proper grasp of pencil; letters the same size or slightly larger than at five and more sloppily written because children are usually in a hurry or experimenting with new letter formation; spontaneous mixing of uppercase and lowercase letters; unpredictable spacing

Favorite themes for children this age:

- Families

- Friends

- Our school

- Workers in our school

- Jobs people do in our community

- Nature topics (such as butterflies, seasons, plants)

- Losing teeth

- Cultural, racial, language, and other differences among people

Provide opportunities for children this age to:

- Do mental mathematics and problem solving after they've mastered the necessary skills with concrete materials

- Do basic computation with money, sometimes using a calculator or computer

- Complete simple worksheets to practice basic computation

- Experiment with reversing operations (+ and -)

- Do lots of measuring using the sand or water table, their feet, and blocks

- Work with manipulatives such as magnets, pulleys, puzzles, interlocking cubes, scoops, funnels, measuring cups, and sand

Seven-Year-Olds

"On a bicycle I traveled over the known world's edge,
and the ground held. I was seven."

An American Childhood | *by Annie Dillard*

———

Years ago, Massachusetts teacher Bob Strachota devised a way to teach soccer to seven-year-olds that shows a clear understanding of the age, plus a streak of genius. Bob divides the field into three equal sections—a midfield and two goal zones. A class of twenty to twenty-two youngsters is first divided in half to make two teams. Each team is then divided into thirds, and a third from each team is assigned to one of three sections of the field. Thus, three to four players on each team are restricted to their third of the field. The play is fast and furious in each section, but as soon as the ball passes over a section line, the players in that section must only watch as play is passed on to the next section.

This adaptation of the game responds, almost poetically, to seven-year-olds' need for restriction, a need related to their tendency toward self-absorption and self-consciousness. "Sevens Soccer" at the Greenfield Center School, where Strachota teaches, enables all sevens to experience a measure of success on the playing field. Without these clear boundaries, many would choose to avoid altogether the perceived risks of actively engaging in the game. Others would dominate the field and show off for anyone watching.

85

Sevens can be extremely moody, sulky, and sometimes depressed. They are often content to spend long periods in their rooms, alone by choice, reading or listening to music or playing with animals or dolls. At school, too, they like to be by themselves and appreciate quiet corners for reading or working. They also like working with a best friend, although relationships may be on one day and off the next.

This is an inward, consolidating period of growth. Sevens have developed a good working concept of right and left and general directionality. Visually, they tend to focus on small details that are close to their eyes. Their tiny printing is anchored to the baseline of the paper, their finger grasp down on the lead of the pencil, their heads resting on their arm or desk as they write, sometimes with one eye closed. Because of their close-up visual concentration, sevens have great difficulty copying from the board, so this task should be minimized.

Sevens are hard workers and often perfectionists. Whereas sixes are fond of the pencil sharpener, sevens adore the eraser. If they make mistakes they will erase and erase, sometimes putting a hole right through the paper. They want to be correct and they want their work to look good, too. Because of this tendency, they take a long time with everything they do and get very upset when not given enough time to finish their work. Timed tests can be extremely upsetting for sevens. Unfortunately, second grade these days is requiring more and more of this type of assessment.

If you schedule a class of seven-year-olds to take a spelling test at the end of the week, requesting that they spell the words correctly and in their best handwriting, you are almost guaranteeing failure. Sevens can do their best work in spelling or in handwriting, but not both at the same time.

Sevens love the routine and structure of school and appreciate their personal relationship with the teacher. Substitute teachers

often feel frustrated with sevens, who constantly tell them, "That's not the way our teacher does it!"

In the classroom, sevens are good listeners and still enjoy being read a story. They show great interest in new words, number relationships, and codes. They like working and talking with one other person (while playing board and card games or working on puzzles) but don't always do well on group projects.

At six, children are noisy, verbal, active, and brash; at seven, they are quieter, more specific in their speech, passive, and sometimes tense. Sevens' industriousness is now concentrated on individual work. They home in on what they can do and practice it over and over. If someone copies their work, seven-year-olds can become extremely upset. Music lessons, often introduced at this age, can be both rewarding and frustrating.

"I quit!" is often heard at home and on the playground, but it's not because sevens don't get their own way, although that's a frequent interpretation. They may walk away from a group game or a family project because of an overwhelming feeling of inferiority. Sevens' feelings need to be protected. Teasing, joking, and especially sarcasm are painful to the seven-year-old. Being laughed at for a wrong answer or a "silly" idea can produce anger and tears.

At six, a child might respond to these feelings with a punch. Seven-year-olds are more apt to drive these feelings deep inside and are less apt to risk themselves the next time they are called on to answer in class or asked to do something. They are hypersensitive to physical ailments as well, both real and imagined.

Seven is an age where children are driven by curiosity and a strong internal desire to discover and invent. As they consolidate logical thinking, they begin to organize their internal mental structures in new ways. Now they can classify spontaneously: "Black bear, brown bear, grizzly bear, koala bear," they chant excitedly. They are intensely interested in how things work and love to take things apart and put them back together again, if they can. Working in a block corner holds as much fascination for the seven as for children at younger ages. Interlocking blocks and other small manipulatives are favorites, and sevens delight in making miniature accessories for their block structures or social studies dioramas.

Sevens are beginning to deal with concepts of time, space, and quantity with increased sophistication. Although they must still act directly on their environment if they are to learn, they are increasingly able to represent their understanding symbolically in writing and drawing. Writing can be a favorite activity when teachers give seven-year-olds extended periods to create their own stories.

Science and social studies take on new meaning as sevens show increasing interest in the world around them. This interest will expand through ages eight, nine, and ten, and children will begin to identify areas of personal enjoyment and concern. It's important for children to study and understand their own city or town before using textbooks to examine desert or mountain villages in foreign countries!

The child's increasing ability to do math without manipulatives, to infer, predict, and estimate, makes mathematical concepts particularly accessible at this age.

Seven is an age of intensity. Individualized activity consolidates new cognitive structures and feelings. A balance between hard work and self-assessment produces a sense of competence, setting the stage for greater self-direction at older ages.

Seven-Year-Olds: Growth Patterns

PHYSICAL	▪ Often keep their eyes focused on a small, close area
	▪ Sometimes tense
	▪ Like confined spaces
	▪ Can be sensitive to many hurts, real and imagined
	▪ Have improved physical abilities (for example, are better at playing sports)
SOCIAL-EMOTIONAL	▪ Inward-looking; sometimes moody, touchy, depressed, sulky, or shy
	▪ May change friendships quickly and feel "nobody likes me"
	▪ Need security and structure; rely on adults for help and constant reassurance
	▪ Don't like taking risks or making mistakes
	▪ Sensitive to others' feelings, but sometimes tattle
	▪ Conscientious and serious; have strong likes and dislikes
	▪ Keep belongings neater at home and school than at six

- Listen well and speak precisely

- Enjoy one-to-one conversations and like to send notes

- Rapidly develop their vocabularies

- Show great interest in meanings of words and enjoy all sorts of codes

- Enjoy repeating tasks and reviewing learning

- Like to work by themselves slowly and finish what they start

- Bothered by mistakes and try hard to make their work perfect

- Good at classifying—sorting buttons, pictures, leaves, shapes, etc.

- Like to be read to

- Enjoy board games as well as computer games

- Enjoy hands-on exploration—taking things apart and discovering how they work

- Increasingly able to reflect on their learning

Seven-Year-Olds in the Classroom

VISION AND **FINE MOTOR ABILITY**	■ Writing, drawing, and numbers are tidy and small, if not microscopic; work with head down on desk, often covering or closing one eye
	■ Find cursive handwriting difficult, even if begun in earlier grades but usually achieve competency by third grade; copying cursive in workbooks is visually easier for them than copying from the board
	■ Anchor their printing and drawing to the baseline; find filling up the line space difficult
	■ Often hold pencil near point with three-fingered, pincer-like grasp that they find difficult to relax
GROSS MOTOR ABILITY	■ Prefer board games to gym games; playground games such as jump rope, four square, and hop-scotch are more popular than team or large-group activities
COGNITIVE GROWTH	■ Need a classroom environment suitable for sustained, quiet work periods
	■ Because of their strong need for routine and clo-sure, need time to finish their work; appreciate a "heads-up" that it's time to prepare for transitions
	■ May find timed tests especially troublesome
	■ Like to work by themselves or in two's

continued on next page

- Enjoy memorization along with codes, puzzles, and other "secrets"

- Comfortable with emphasis on high-quality products and proper display of work

- Like to repeat tasks

- Like to review learning verbally or frequently touch base in other ways with their teacher

- Enjoy inquiry activities; often work well in "discovery" centers; like to collect and sort

- Not fully able to read without vocalizing—still sometimes whisper to themselves during "silent" reading

- Frequently change friends but accept teacher's seating assignments

- Prefer working and playing alone or with one friend

- Find classroom changes upsetting; need teachers to prepare them in advance when substitutes will take over the classroom

- Need humor and games to help moderate their seriousness

- Can get sick from worrying about tests, assignments, etc.

- Changeable; close communication between teachers and parents helps ensure their needs are understood

Seven-Year-Olds: Curriculum

Provide opportunities for children this age to:

- Do less partner reading and more individual reading (their greater strength at this age)

- Continue phonics work; ready for intense phonics instruction in small groups

- Do written reading comprehension assignments

Expect from these children:

- *Writing:* Longer stories with beginning, middle, and end, including "chapter" books in some cases; great interest in the story line; tendency to include every-thing from "breakfast to bed"; writing before drawing and sometimes even writing without drawing; readi-ness to begin nonfiction writing as a way to show learning from science or social studies investigations

- *Spelling:* Correct spelling slowly emerging from transitional spelling; increased phonetic and sight word fluency; ease in learning capitalization and punctuation; readiness for formal spelling program (teachers should still accept "invented" spelling because children still do not see revision as neces-sary or important)

- *Writing Themes:* Family; friends; sleeping over; losing teeth; trips; pets (often including first stories about the death of pets); nightmares; worries about the death of family members, illness, war, famine, or other serious issues

continued on next page

- *Handwriting:* Very tight pencil grasp down on the shaft of the pencil, often right on the lead; their letters are often microscopic in size and anchored to the baseline; not a good age at which to introduce cursive handwriting (better for younger or older children)

Favorite themes for children this age:

- Our neighborhood

- How systems work (plumbing, lighting, heating in our school; how we get our milk; how the cafeteria works)

- Jobs people do

- Things we are good at

- Cultural and racial diversity and discrimination

- Natural science topics (pond, forest, meadow, etc.)

Provide opportunities for children this age to:

- Do more computation with money and time

- Do more complex mental mathematics and solve equations

- Work with fractions by measuring, weighing, and comparing

- Experiment with symmetry and other simple geometry by using, for example, unit blocks or pattern blocks

- Do simple computation with multiplication; do division based on experience with concrete materials

- Continue practicing mathematical skills by playing games

Eight-Year-Olds

"Mothers for miles around worried about Zuckerman's swing.
They feared some child would fall off. But no child ever did.
Children almost always hang onto things tighter
than their parents think they will."

Charlotte's Web | *by E. B. White*

"Teacher, we have a great idea!"

Watch out! Here come the eight-year-olds—full of energy, imagination, and little sense of their own limits.

"We have this great idea to do a play about Rosa Parks and we have all the clothes at home and we're going to bring them in tomorrow and we can use your desk for the bus and we can make tickets and charge admission and we'll put it on tomorrow . . . OK?"

There's no thought of a script, assigning parts, rehearsal schedules, the hard work of learning lines, practice, set, and production. It's all a blur of enthusiasm tempered by only a vague understanding of how things get done.

The job of the second or third grade teacher is to harness that eight-year-old energy and give it some direction and focus. Throughout the year, teachers need to help children cut work down to bite-size pieces. This includes homework assignments, which should never be longer than a half-hour in duration and should be limited in scope and expectations. Children at this age need to experience "incremental success" in their schoolwork—success in gradually increasing quantities and levels of complexity—so that they will continue feeling motivated and excited.

Eight-year-olds tend to gravitate toward their own gender when making choices about working and playing with others. Boys tend to be fascinated by the world of "smutty" jokes at this age, but both boys and girls enjoy virtually any kind of humor, including riddles, limericks, and knock-knock jokes.

A key developmental struggle for eight-year-olds is gaining competence over the tools of their trade. At school, this means industrious efforts in such areas as handwriting, handcrafts, computer skills, drawing and sketching, and simple geometry. But when accomplishments don't come easily or quickly, the children feel a strong sense of inferiority. Patience is not common in eight-year-olds. Again, assignments (in handwriting or spelling, for instance) need to be short and to the point. Drafts of children's work as well as beautiful, finished work should be liberally displayed in the classroom so that children can see the range of effort required to make progress toward mastery in a certain area. Children also benefit by graphing or charting their progress in certain areas, which helps combat that feeling of "I'll never get it . . . I'll never be able to do this."

"I'm bored!" is a common complaint of the eight-year-old. Adult translation: "This is too hard!" Look beyond these words to what the children are showing you in their work. Encouragement and redirection go a long way. For example, to a child who's beginning to become frustrated with a math problem, a teacher could say, "It *is* a hard problem. But if you keep thinking and trying new things, I bet you'll get it." A child who's ready to quit after unsuccessful tries might be helped with a firm but gentle redirection: "Try it this way now. Then let's talk about what happens."

Often, parents and teachers lament about an eight-year-old, "He could do it if he only tried. He's lazy and unmotivated. He never sticks to any one thing for more than a day." Actually, the eight-year-old is exploring his potential. He may be struggling with feelings of inferiority as he tries out one new area after another in an expanding awareness of the broader world. This uncertainty will reach a peak at nine.

Eight-Year-Olds: Growth Patterns

PHYSICAL

- Full of energy; do things in a hurry
- Need physical release through time to play outdoors
- Somewhat awkward
- Visually, focus well on both near and far objects

SOCIAL-EMOTIONAL

- Enjoy socializing and sharing humor
- Love group activities and cooperative work, preferably with peers of the same gender
- Adjust well to change; bounce back quickly from mistakes or disappointments
- Form larger friendship groups than at seven

LANGUAGE

- Like to talk, explain ideas, and use rapidly expanding vocabularies
- Tend to exaggerate
- Listen well, but they have so many ideas that they may not always remember what they've heard

- Have limited attention span but do become engrossed in the activity at hand; love to socialize at the same time

- Industrious, impatient, and full of ideas; work quickly and often take on more than they can handle

- Can use geometric solids, math counters, rulers, balance scales, and other manipulatives to explain their thinking and problem solving in concrete ways

- Beginning to master handwriting, handcrafts, computers, and drawing

Eight-Year-Olds in the Classroom

VISION AND FINE MOTOR ABILITY	▪ Better control of eyes and hands enables children to copy from the board and learn cursive writing; they love to practice writing but often produce sloppy work ▪ Pencil grasp should now be the same as an adult's; if not, they may still need a pencil grip placed on their pencil to help correct their grasp
GROSS MOTOR ABILITY	▪ Often experience a growth spurt; restless and need lots of physical activity; short exercise breaks (even in the classroom) help concentration ▪ Love group games on the playground; gravitate toward same-gender activities, so the teacher should lead whole-class games such as tag and soccer ▪ Play hard and tire quickly; benefit more from several short play breaks than one long one
COGNITIVE GROWTH	▪ Very industrious, but often exaggerate their own ability and have trouble knowing their limits; more short assignments, rather than a few long ones, build confidence through success in small doses ▪ Enjoy responsibility, although they do not always successfully complete tasks ▪ Care about both the process and the product of schoolwork; want their peers' approval as much as their teacher's *continued on next page*

- Usually organize work well, though tend to be sloppy; some need the teacher's help with organizational strategies

- Show increasing interest in rules, logic, how things are put together, how things work, the natural world, and classification

- Can handle increasingly complex tasks but tire easily; may give up but soon want to try again

- Work best in groups at tables or at pushed-together desks; teachers should change groupings frequently throughout the year

- Prefer working and playing with peers of the same gender

- Respond well to class projects and traditions that build a sense of unity and cohesion

- As they develop a growing sense of moral responsibility beyond themselves, they become more interested in fairness issues and may argue about them

- Like stories that concern fairness and justice

- Enjoy studying other cultures

Eight-Year-Olds: Curriculum

Provide opportunities for children this age to:

- Work in groups reading trade books (which are good for children at all ages) or in core reading programs keyed to their ability levels and organized around their interests

- Begin reading independently and doing simple independent assignments (such as making book covers, conducting interviews, and building dioramas); teachers should design these projects specifically to spur children's interest in reading and to let them show their comprehension

- Be read to from books with lengthier chapters and more advanced themes

Expect from these children:

- *Writing:* Quite lengthy stories with increasingly descriptive language; interest in diverse kinds of writing such as poetry, newspaper articles, and cartoons; fascination with the "breakfast to bed" story line—tendency to provide more detail than any reader (except the author) would care to know; beginning understanding of the importance of making drafts and revising

- *Spelling:* Increasing ability to spell correctly; readiness to learn compound words, dictionary use, and alphabetical order; skill development to a level that makes lingering phonetic mistake patterns and real difficulty in spelling more obvious

continued on next page

- *Writing Themes:* Adventure and "breakfast to bed" stories, animals, sports with friends and heroes, unicorns and other mythical beasts, stories based on cartoons, poetry about nature and the seasons, nonfiction writing that shows learning from concrete science and social studies investigations

- *Handwriting:* Good posture, good pencil grasp, and fluid movement of arm and hand across the page; readiness to learn cursive handwriting and to practice extensively; although easily frustrated, enjoyment of writing practice and motivation to become competent

Favorite themes for children this age:

- Our neighborhood, our community (interdependence)

- Community institutions (bank, newspaper, radio)

- Long ago or far away (but not both)

- Topics in nature (trees, rocks, animals, etc.)

- Cultural and racial diversity

Provide opportunities for children this age to:

- Solve math problems using all four operations, as well as borrowing and carrying

- Study fractions by measuring, weighing, and doing some pencil and paper tasks

- Explore geometric patterns constructed with pencil and paper

- Use games as a way to practice math strategies

Nine-Year-Olds

*"My ninth year was certainly more exciting
than any of the others. But not all of it was exactly
what you would call fun."*

Danny, the Champion of the World | *by Roald Dahl*

———

"I hate living in Greenfield! It is so boring! It isn't a city town. It isn't a country town either. It isn't a suburb town and it isn't the kind of town you'd visit your Aunt Mabel in. It is a medium sized town with a few country back roads, a few corner stores, a few movie theaters, some restaurants and many houses. It doesn't sound too bad you say? It is. The trouble is there's nothing to do! The most exciting thing that's ever happened to me in Greenfield was a train derailment. And it turned out o.k. You see, if you go to Boston you have the swan boats, you go to California, you have the beach, you go to Greenfield you have . . . um–um . . . see what I mean. That's why I wish Greenfield were better."

I've never forgotten this essay from Kate Arsenault, now an adult. With its exclamation marks and sardonic humor, it's a perfect expression of the often confused and troubled age of nine. The enthusiasm of eight often turns into dark brooding and worrying at nine—worrying about world events, about the health of parents, about moving away, about losing best friends, about changing schools. Teachers notice these thinly veiled themes again and again

107

in children's fiction writing. Sometimes the deep seriousness of these social concerns can bring a twinkle to the adult eye. One nine-year-old worked diligently on her protest poster on a Saturday morning: "Save the Elephants—Ban Ivory Soap."

Fourth grade now tends to be a "benchmark" grade for state tests in at least two subject areas. But test-taking is a difficult task for nine-year-olds; in fact, it can be a disaster. It's easy to see how the well-known dip in fourth grade test scores could relate to the anxiousness of nines. The best test takers in the world are the risk takers; nines are anything but good risk takers. Teachers at this level see children finish their tests early simply because they put down any answer, rather than think through what they know. Others get only halfway through because they get stuck trying to figure out one right answer, refusing to be wrong. Nines need many opportunities to practice test-taking before it's time for the real thing. Modeling and role-playing can defuse the anxiety that tests create.

Compared with younger and older schoolmates, nines tend to learn better on their own as they gain mastery of basic skills. They're gaining a more solid understanding of key cognitive concepts such as multiplication, spelling patterns, and the scientific process. Younger children enjoy experimenting with these processes, but nines now take care with the final product. They will work hard on a science report on butterflies and study for weekly spelling tests or a chapter test in math.

Nothing is fair to the nine-year-old, who is struggling with the cognitive task of understanding ethical behavior at a new level. Why do children die? Why is there AIDS? Why are there poor people? How come a few people have all the money? Nines often feel they are singled out for unfair treatment by a teacher, parent, or sports coach. Sometimes these complaints are a way for nines to express a growing sense of peer importance and group solidarity: "You're never fair to us . . . we never get to do anything." This growing peer solidarity of nines can be channeled into wonderful

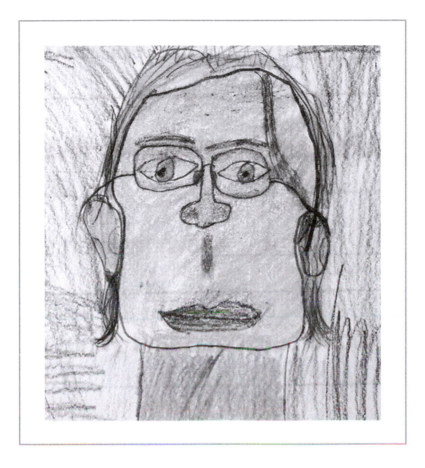

club activities. Children enjoy gathering to play chess or to share their collections of rocks or stamps.

Nines complain about their aches and pains, their cuts and bruises, and their hurt feelings. Nail biting, hair twisting, and other outlets for tension are common. Teachers of nine-year-olds in third and fourth grade need a sense of humor and a determined lightness to challenge the sometimes deadly seriousness of the age. Positive language is also essential for children's growth. An ounce of negative criticism is greatly magnified by the nine-year-old. So is an ounce of encouragement.

Nine-Year-Olds: Growth Patterns

PHYSICAL

- Better coordinated

- Like to push their physical limits; tire easily

- Complain about aches, pains, injuries, and hurt feelings

- May twist hair, bite nails, or purse lips to relieve tension

SOCIAL-EMOTIONAL

- More individualistic

- Often feel worried or anxious

- Impatient

- Often complain about fairness issues

- Critical of self and others (including adults)

- Can be sullen, moody, aloof, and negative; often say "I hate it," "It's boring," etc.

LANGUAGE

- Love descriptive language, word play, and new vocabulary

- Sometimes revert to baby talk

- Enjoy exaggeration, "dirty" jokes, and graffiti

- Industrious and intellectually curious, but less imaginative than at eight

- Beginning to see the "bigger world," including issues of fairness and justice

- Able to manage more than one concept at a time, such as "long ago and far away"

- Have trouble understanding abstractions, such as large numbers, long periods of time, or vast areas of space

Nine-Year-Olds in the Classroom

VISION AND FINE MOTOR ABILITY	■ With better coordination and control, show more interest in details
	■ Can fully master cursive handwriting, although they may need help relaxing their overly tight pencil grasp
	■ Benefit from practice with a variety of fine motor tools and tasks (weaving, knitting, carving, drawing, etc.)
	■ Able to copy from the board, recopy assignments, and produce beautiful final drafts
GROSS MOTOR ABILITY	■ Like to push their physical limits, whether challenging themselves, racing each other, or trying to beat the clock
	■ Still learning physical control; have trouble staying within boundaries
	■ Boys love to roughhouse, tumbling and wrestling like puppies
	■ Complain of and sometimes exaggerate physical hurts
	■ Restless; can't sit still for long
COGNITIVE GROWTH	■ Need homework related specifically to the next day's work; often ask the teacher, "Why do we have to do this?"

continued on next page

- Looking hard (often anxiously) for explanations of facts, how things work, why things happen as they do; a good age for scientific exploration

- Reading to learn, instead of learning to read: If reading ability has kept pace with grade level expectations, they can read for information in books and newspapers and on websites

- Take pride in attention to detail and finished work, but may jump quickly between interests

- Like to work with a partner of their choice—usually of the same gender; may begin to form cliques

- Can work in groups but may spend more time arguing about facts, rules, and directions than doing the actual activity

- Very competitive; need their teacher's sense of lightness and fun to help them relax in class and on the playground

- Like to negotiate—this is the age of "Let's make a deal"

- Generally worried and anxious; need adult patience and clarity when giving directions or setting expectations

- Very self-critical; sarcastic humor from adults can be very hurtful

- Tend to give up on tasks; encouragement to try again builds up their fragile sense of competence

- Exasperation on their teacher's part leads to more complaints, whining, or moodiness; laughing with nines is the best medicine

Nine-Year-Olds: Curriculum

Provide opportunities for children this age to:

- Continue working in reading groups

- Tackle assignments that involve beginning research tasks and use of related reading material

- Intensively develop dictionary skills introduced at earlier ages

- Volunteer to read orally during read-aloud

- Explore poetry seriously throughout the year

Expect from these children:

- *Writing:* Readiness for emphasis on first draft and revision process; ability to absorb teaching about descriptive writing, character development, plot, cohesiveness and believability; frequent episodes of "writer's block"

- *Spelling:* Improving use of dictionary; improving first-draft spelling; fewer mistakes with spelling in journals and subject writing; readiness for weekly spelling tests; mastery of basic capitalization and punctuation

- *Writing Themes:* Moving away, divorce, death, disease, and other worries; world issues; poetry about feelings and darker themes

- *Handwriting:* Increasingly fluent cursive; beginning use of cursive in day-to-day assignments and spontaneous writing; much neater writing than at eight

Favorite themes for children this age:

- Our country and the world

- Long ago and far away

- History of cultures

- Racial and ethnic diversity

- Environmental concerns in the immediate environment (for example, air or water pollution)

- Literary characters or a theme emerging from a particular book

Provide opportunities for children this age to:

- Practice division by measuring, working with fractions, doing surveys, and graphing as well as through experimenting with standard algorithms

- Work extensively with word problems

- Compute with money and begin learning about decimals

- Practice multiplication tables

A Final Thought on Nine-Year-Olds

The internal emotional roller coaster that some children experience when they are nine is poignantly captured in the following poem by Billy Collins.

On Turning Ten

by Billy Collins

The whole idea of it makes me feel
like I'm coming down with something,
something worse than any stomach ache
or the headaches I get from reading in bad light—
a kind of measles of the spirit,
a mumps of the psyche,
a disfiguring chicken pox of the soul.

You tell me it is too early to be looking back,
but that is because you have forgotten
the perfect simplicity of being one
and the beautiful complexity introduced by two.
But I can lie on my bed and remember every digit.
At four I was an Arabian wizard.
I could make myself invisible
by drinking a glass of milk a certain way.
At seven I was a soldier, at nine a prince.

But now I am mostly at the window
watching the late afternoon light.
Back then it never fell so solemnly
against the side of my tree house,
and my bicycle never leaned against the garage
as it does today,
all the dark blue speed drained out of it.

This is the beginning of sadness, I say to myself,
as I walk through the universe in my sneakers.
It is time to say good-bye to my imaginary friends,
time to turn the first big number.

It seems only yesterday I used to believe
there was nothing under my skin but light.
If you cut me I would shine.
But now when I fall upon the sidewalks of life,
I skin my knees. I bleed.

"On Turning Ten" is from *The Art of Drowning*, by Billy Collins, © 1995.
Reprinted by permission of the University of Pittsburgh Press.

Ten-Year-Olds

"Mrs. Hanson told Diane and me to get our folders and place them on our desks. I made a pretty semicircle with mine. I was glad I had only good papers for my parents to see."

Nothing's Fair in Fifth Grade | *by Barthe DeClements*

———

"Can we stay in today and finish the book? Please!" "Will you read more this afternoon, Mrs. Goodwin? We promise to do our math for homework if you would. This story is so awesome!"

"Yeah," comes the chorus of hushed voices.

"Well . . . all right, children . . . but just one more chapter," yields Mrs. Goodwin, silently delighting in one of those magic moments of teaching, one she will always treasure about this class.

The children settle back in, sprawling on the carpet, or chins on hands at their desks; two girls lean against Mrs. Goodwin as she reads from her comfy chair. The story continues.

Such scenes are repeated often when children are ten. To exaggerate a little, here is the golden end of childhood. At ten, children find comfort in themselves, their teachers, their parents, and even their siblings. They relax in their childhood, gathering strength for the impending storm of adolescence and consolidating their gains from their early years. You can see this clearly in the cognitive choices that children make in school. Tens concentrate on, even relish, producing tangible products that display their competence—book reports, theme reports, beginning research writing, and scientific documentation.

These industrious children are also able to easily share their knowledge with their classmates and work well on group projects. This is the ideal age for the class play or trip, and tens can often help elevens and even twelves in cooperative pursuits because of their relative calmness and instinct for cooperation.

At ten, children seem to be at their most actively receptive as learners of factual information. This is usually a good time to master the multiplication tables that have been such a struggle until now. It's an age for state capitals, presidents, principal products of major nations, exports and imports, and poetry and speech memorization. Education about the human body, sex, childbirth, and child rearing (as determined by the school's curriculum policy) can be more effective now than a year or two later when children are more self-conscious about their bodies. The facts are more easily taught and remembered, and boys and girls tend to work well together.

Children know all the rules at ten, thanks to their facile memories. Board games and games of strategy are great favorites, and tens are likely to be in mutual agreement about how to play, rather than endlessly arguing about rules. It's a wonderful age at which to teach or reteach mediation, to introduce or reintroduce problem-solving formats in class meeting, to teach governmental structures and scientific principles. All these will be challenged at eleven, argued with at twelve, and rebelled against at thirteen. But ten is a great time for initial introduction and general acceptance, which plant the seeds for the more formal and more abstract cognitive challenges ahead.

Just as children at every chronological age will vary somewhat from the typical developmental picture for that age, not all ten-year-olds will perfectly fit this generally happy picture all of the time. Some children at ten will have issues with friendships, homework, or subjects that are hard for them, or they will struggle with difficult medical or family dilemmas. But there is a sturdiness about ten that can help the children get through these situations. That sturdiness is observable in many fifth grade classrooms.

Outdoor play is as critical for preadolescent children as it is for children in early childhood (see "Exercise" in the "Developmental Considerations" section). Schools that have eliminated recess have taken away children's inalienable right and undeniable need to play. Breaks are especially important to these industrious ten-year-olds, allowing them to bounce back from fatigue and do even more schoolwork.

Tens especially love group games outdoors. They can learn, and usually enjoy, cooperative and noncompetitive activities as well as more traditional and competitive games like kickball, tag, and dodgeball. Boys and girls play well together in either kind of activity. Group initiatives and challenges have great success at this age, so it's a good time for formal outdoor education like a ropes course challenge or overnight camping. Children often have their fondest memories of weeks at summer camp when they were ten.

Ordering their world is central to ten-year-olds. Enjoy the clean bedroom, the orderly classroom, and the relative absence of arguments. Observe and capitalize on children's interest in classification and seriation: they love rock collections, sets of baseball and superhero cards, doll and teddy bear and unicorn collections, jewelry boxes, secret compartments. Teach about phylum and genus and other ways of organizing the world. Teach beginning genetics, the value of repeating experiments and testing variables. Teach tens about attributes and combinations of attributes to describe different phenomena. The world is theirs to organize.

Ten-Year-Olds: Growth Patterns

PHYSICAL	■ Large muscles are developing quickly
	■ Desperately need outdoor time and physical challenge
	■ Often write more sloppily than at nine
	■ Snacks and rest periods benefit their rapidly growing bodies
SOCIAL-EMOTIONAL	■ Generally content; enjoy family, peers, and teachers
	■ Friendly, generally happy; quick to anger and quick to forgive
	■ Work very well in groups; enjoy clubs, activities, and team sports
	■ Usually truthful; developing more mature sense of right and wrong
	■ Highly sensitive to and able to resolve questions of fairness and other social issues
	■ Able to enjoy cooperative and competitive activities
LANGUAGE	■ Listen well
	■ Read voraciously
	■ Expressive and talkative; like to explain things

- Very good at memorizing facts

- Increasingly able to think abstractly; enjoy rules and logic; good at solving problems

- Enjoy collecting, classifying, and organizing

- Can concentrate for long periods

- Take pride in schoolwork

Ten-Year-Olds in the Classroom

VISION AND FINE MOTOR ABILITY	■ Able to focus well on both the board and close-up written work
	■ Can pay attention to spelling, dictation, and penmanship all at once, but work may be somewhat sloppy as they learn to integrate these skills
	■ Particularly enjoy tracing and copying as fine motor skills strengthen; making maps and drawing cartoons provide excellent fine motor practice
	■ Ready to start using tools such as compasses, protractors, rulers, and templates; need plenty of practice time
GROSS MOTOR ABILITY	■ Need a great deal of physical activity; large muscles for jumping, running, and other big movements are developing quickly, although upper body strength is generally undeveloped
	■ Extra recess and play time are a must, or their energy may spill over into acting out in the classroom
	■ Love group games, relays, group initiatives, class outings, ropes courses, double Dutch jump rope clubs, team sports, and other organized activities
COGNITIVE GROWTH	■ Highly productive with schoolwork; usually conscientious with homework; pay close attention to form, structure, directions, and organization

continued on next page

- Receptive learners; very good at memorization; love geography, world records, facts about sports and TV programs, and activities requiring memory skills (such as spelling, math, and certain computer and electronic games)

- Enjoy choral reading, singing, poetry, and plays

- With concrete organizational skills at their peak, enjoy classification, seriation, and exactness; enjoy and learn much from working on collections and science and math projects

- Basically cooperative nature is conducive to group activity, whole class cohesion, and collaborative learning; ten is a good age for learning peer mediation and conflict resolution

- Quite concerned with friendship and fairness issues; teams, groups, games, and competitions help them practice social interaction

- Generally satisfied with their own abilities; happy and flexible

- Eager to reach out to others, such as through community service or tutoring younger children

- Enjoy being noticed and rewarded for their efforts; respond well to the teacher's "noticing" language; for example, "Claire, I noticed that you were frustrated with that math problem at first, but you kept trying different strategies until you got it!"

- Quick tempers may lead to physical outbursts and tears, but problems are usually quickly and easily solved

Ten-Year-Olds: Curriculum

Provide opportunities for children this age to:

- Read, memorize, and recite poetry, do choral readings, and put on plays

- Read trade books centered on themes

- Read independently and indulge their desire to devour one book after another; read more and do fewer book projects

- Enjoy comic books

Expect from these children:

- *Writing:* Readiness to write lengthy chapter books, longer poems, first research papers, pieces about famous people—all usually filled with light and descriptive language; more frequent use of humor; more use of dialogue; description of realistic inter-action between characters

- *Spelling:* Enjoy memorizing how to spell difficult words and using the words, properly spelled, in day-to-day writing

- *Writing Themes:* Friends, friends, and more friends in many adventures; time travel; writing letters to request information; writing notes to friends; writing reports

- *Handwriting:* Fluent cursive (keyboarding helps those having great difficulty)

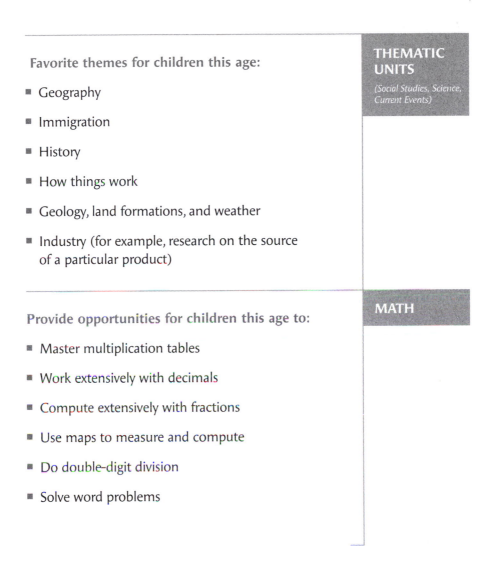

Favorite themes for children this age:

- Geography

- Immigration

- History

- How things work

- Geology, land formations, and weather

- Industry (for example, research on the source of a particular product)

Provide opportunities for children this age to:

- Master multiplication tables

- Work extensively with decimals

- Compute extensively with fractions

- Use maps to measure and compute

- Do double-digit division

- Solve word problems

Eleven-Year-Olds

"Phillip nodded. 'For a girl, you take jokes better than anybody.' Suddenly he pointed down the road and this time the yellow bus was really on its way. He smiled a dimpled smile and I remembered why he's the cutest boy in the J. T. Williams School."

Phillip Hall Likes Me, I Reckon Maybe | *by Bette Greene*

It's near the end of the morning's math lesson. The children are growing fidgety, but the teacher presses on.

"What's another name for a parallelogram? . . . Yes, Max?"

"It's past time for recess. We're missing our recess!"

A chorus of agreement greets the teacher.

Finally out at recess, the fifth and sixth graders mill around on the kickball field.

"Same teams as yesterday!" yells one girl.

"No way!" screams another, "You smushed us yesterday."

"Yeah, but Jamal isn't here today, so that makes it even," says the first girl.

"Yeah, but look who you got today," says the other. The arguments continue. They use up ten full minutes of their precious recess time making up teams. No one seems to mind.

As children move from ten to eleven, major changes begin to take place. In their cognitive growth, children seem to be challenging all their assumptions about the world. Cognitive structures in the brain seem to be rearranging themselves at the same speed with which the body is beginning to transform.

Eleven, of course, marks the beginning of adolescence, especially for girls, whose physical growth is generally way ahead of the boys'. The onset of menstruation is common at eleven, the average being at twelve. As the girls' bodies change, emotional sensitivity and volatility increase. The clear physical difference between boys and girls leads to natural separation between them in the classroom and on the playground.

Although mixed-gender activity still happens and should certainly still be encouraged, it is not as spontaneously attractive for children as it was when they were ten. Watch how children come to the meeting circle or to a game, the boys on one side, the girls on another. Boys are watching the girls change and wondering when they themselves will begin to change. Both genders are interested in knowledge about sex and changing bodies, and this education should continue for both (as determined by the school's curriculum policy).

It's common for eleven-year-olds to question many of the adult judgments they have previously accepted. Teachers may face challenges on nearly every topic: assignments; homework; rules in the classroom; interpretations of literature, history, and governmental policy; adult authority in general. Although not always polite or

on target, these challenges should be seen and addressed as signs of cognitive as well as social–emotional growth.

Elevens are engaged in significant changes in their learning approaches and strategies. Their awkwardness and sometimes apparent rudeness commonly cause conflict between parents and children as well as teachers and children unless the developmental issues are understood. Elevens are often genuinely surprised that adults take offense at their challenges, and they are easily hurt. Parents and teachers also struggle because just a little while ago, at ten, these children were so easy to get along with, such delightful and reasonable friends to have around.

"Saving face" is very important for the easily embarrassed eleven-year-old, even in seemingly innocuous situations. It's especially important to try to avoid correcting the eleven-year-old in front of peers. Instead, find a time and place away from the group. When possible, waiting awhile after the incident itself also helps.

The growing cognitive strength of the eleven-year-old is fed by learning new and demanding skills in research, such as footnoting, bibliography, and scientific notation. It's also a good age for learning on the computer. Elevens are especially turned off by traditional workbooks and other packaged programs that claim to teach "skills used in real life." Instead, they need the opportunity to interview the fire chief, take notes at a local meeting, or write a letter to a map company or local corporation.

Although their new skills in these more adult realms may be crude and tentative at first, elevens are motivated by the opportunity to try out brand new arenas of knowledge. Foreign language, music, and new forms of artistic expression are also attractive. These challenges aren't met without complaint. Easily frustrated, the eleven-year-old may fuss to their teacher that some schoolwork is too hard, while telling their parents how cool the new subject is, or vice versa. For example, something as hard as written dictation can be outwardly hated but inwardly cherished as a delicious intellectual challenge.

Girls at eleven are at the height of forming cliques, which can result in a great deal of cruelty as well as wonderful friendships. A teacher's role in dealing with cliques is a delicate balance between letting girls work things out for themselves and providing direct mediation. My experience is that if three girls can't solve a problem within a ten-minute time limit, teacher intervention is necessary.

Sports and outdoor activity are important to elevens but often include arguments about team effort and the interpretation of rules. Elevens often focus on their own personal skill development in a sport and constantly compare themselves with the best athletes. Some will drop out of competitive sports around this age as competition gets increasingly serious and the skills more difficult. Teachers and coaches can encourage continued participation by focusing on effort rather than perfection. Trying hard needs to be rewarded as much as scoring.

Changing bodies also affect some girls' willingness to continue in individual activities such as dance, gymnastics, or swimming. Boys struggle with clumsiness in athletics at this age (as well as at twelve and thirteen) as they begin experiencing marked growth spurts. For both boys and girls, muscles don't keep pace with bones, and aches and pains at night and complaints on the playground and in the classroom are common.

At eleven, the awkwardness of adolescence is just beginning, both physically and emotionally. It's a time when feelings and relationships are seldom clear or simple. Teachers and parents need to see through children's language, facial expressions, moods, and intentions and understand that behind them is the child's beginning quest to establish independence and identity—the chief task of adolescence.

Eleven-Year-Olds: Growth Patterns

PHYSICAL

- Restless and very energetic

- Need lots of food, physical activity, and sleep

- Experience more colds, flu, ear infections, etc.

- Many girls experience an early adolescent growth spurt and sexual maturation; some boys begin rapidly growing taller

SOCIAL-EMOTIONAL

- Moody, self-absorbed, and sensitive

- Like to challenge rules, argue, and test limits; may be cruel; sometimes physically aggressive

- Worry more about who's "in" and who's "out" than when they were younger

- Need lots of time to talk with peers; heavy users of the phone, cell phone, instant messaging, and email

- Impulsive—often talk before thinking

- Often behave best when away from home

- Have trouble making decisions

- Need adult empathy, humor, and sensitivity to help them cope with their rapidly changing minds and bodies

- Enjoy arguing and debating

- Appreciate humor

- Imitate adult language

- Would rather learn new skills than review or improve previous work

- Becoming more adept at abstract thinking—for example, they can understand ideas such as "justice"

- With improving reasoning skills, they can establish and modify rules and develop hypotheses

- Increasingly able to see the world from various perspectives

Eleven-Year-Olds in the Classroom

VISION AND FINE MOTOR ABILITY	■ Highly improved fine motor skills lead to more confidence in exploring delicate work (for example, calligraphy, linoleum block printing, and Japanese brush painting); art is an important vehicle to greater focus in reading and math ■ May complain of headaches and read only for short periods of time; music may aid their concentration ■ Often enjoy handwork (weaving, braiding, sewing; etc.), which may aid concentration and serve as an outlet for stress ■ Love computer games and being on the computer in general, sometimes as a stress reducer or, in the case of email and text messaging, a social outlet; adults should help make sure that social use of the computer does not contribute to problems with cliques, bullying, or other inappropriate behaviors or put children at risk in any way
GROSS MOTOR ABILITY	■ Motor skills (such as throwing, catching, and kicking) improve rapidly; they like to measure their individual best ■ "Quiet time" in school day gives needed physical rest, as well as a break from academics and intense social-emotional dynamics
COGNITIVE GROWTH	■ Developing new abilities in deductive reasoning, making this a good age for scientific study, mathematical problem solving, invention, and debate, but hands-on learning is still critical for most ■ Learn well in collaborative groups

continued on next page

continued on next page

- Self-absorbed and interested in imagining themselves in adult roles; this makes history, biography, and current events exciting

- Like "adult" academic tasks such as researching, interviewing, footnoting, and creating a bibliography

- Enjoy board games, intellectual puzzles, brain teasers, and even tests

- Usually challenged rather than defeated by reasonably hard work; need help with time-management and homework skills

- May show interest in and facility for languages, music, or mechanics; need time to explore these areas

- Interested in learning about older and very young people

- Desire to test limits and rules is an important developmental milestone, not a personal attack on the teacher; class meetings, peer mediation, student councils, and cross-age tutoring can be highly effective in resolving issues

- Love the challenge of competition; prefer team sports and getting better at playing as a team

- Teachers can help with inclusion/exclusion issues by changing learning groups to adjust the social mix

- "Saving face" is important; not necessary for the teacher to "win" arguments; giving children private, physical space to think things over helps resolve problems peacefully

- Teacher empathy, a light attitude, and a sense of humor help elevens take themselves less seriously

Eleven-Year-Olds: Curriculum

READING

Provide opportunities for children this age to:

- Take on week-long reading assignments, still using trade books

- Do more nonfiction reading tied to subjects that interest them

- Read biographies

- Read to children in younger grades

WRITING

Expect from these children:

- *Writing:* Willingness to practice, although revision can be a struggle; writing that incorporates personal interests and is more adult-like in plot, character development, and style; very rudimentary research reports; much enjoyment of poetry writing, cartooning, and journaling

- *Spelling:* Ease and accuracy for some children, with most enjoying the challenge of spelling difficult words; readiness to learn more dictionary skills

- *Writing Themes:* For most, blood and gore, fantasy, science fiction, love and romance; for advanced writers, experimentation with a variety of personally compelling themes

- *Handwriting:* Functional cursive for most

Favorite themes for children this age:

- Games

- History

- Biography

- Government

- Community service

- Physical development and body systems

- Plant growth and other forms of measurable, systematic development

Provide opportunities for children this age to:

- Solve complicated word problems

- Study probability and statistics through real-world problems

- Use calculators and computers

- Work on speed and accuracy in computations

- Work with percentages

Twelve-Year-Olds

"I am not a nut. I am a pioneer."

The Real Me | *by Betty Miles*

———

Junior highs that include grades seven, eight, and nine; middle schools with grades six, seven, and eight; schools that are K–8 —we've tried them all during the past forty years, yet we're still trying to figure out how best to reach and teach the twelve-year-old child. Teachers and educators have yet to come up with the perfect environment and program for early adolescence. Twelves, caught up in the world of lockers and fifty-minute classes, are often lost and confused, scared and alone. But in self-contained classrooms, they can appear bored and aloof, disengaged and challenging to adult authority.

The truth may be that there is no perfect place for twelves. For most of my career, I have maintained that twelves (and thirteens and fourteens for that matter) probably do not belong in formal school environments at all, but in some kind of cross between summer camp and the Civilian Conservation Corps camps of the Great Depression—plenty of physical activity, structured groups, and time with peers, with a little formal education thrown in. Of course this will never happen, so success in the school world for children from twelve to fourteen depends on the flexibility of teachers and administrators in creating environments and curricula that can respond to the developmental chaos of these early adolescent years.

143

The primary developmental issue at twelve is the confusing struggle for identity: The child/not-child begins the search for solid, meaningful relationships. As the search intensifies, twelves' greatest need is to be with their friends. Teachers and parents take a back seat on the long ride toward the driver's license and the independent association with friends it represents. Minutes turn to hours on the telephone and computer and in front of the mirror. Twelves define themselves by jackets, hairstyles, shoes, CDs, iPods, movies, TV preferences, sports teams, the mall, the dance rage, what older kids are doing. School becomes the place to be, but not always for our intended purposes.

On the other hand, twelves can also become deeply invested with their peers in purposeful schoolwork. Twelves are excited and challenged by lengthy homework assignments and projects that culminate in visible products: reports with beautiful covers or illustrations; skits about famous people in history, complete with elaborate costumes and props; topographical maps made in three dimensions with chicken wire, papier-mâché, and paint; scientific models with working parts; computer programs that stump or amaze the class. Research projects, current events, environmental issues and causes, community service projects, scientific experiments, major art projects, and dramatic productions can attract and engage the twelve-year-old.

Emotionally, twelves are changeable, unpredictable, and often very hard to read. Sometimes, they want fervently to do their schoolwork as part of a group; other times, they want just as fervently to pursue their learning individually. They often say "That's not what I meant at all!" when a teacher misreads a tone of voice or an offhand, seemingly rude comment. At home, children may seem more introverted and moody, communicate in monosyllables and grunts, and withdraw as they sort out their feelings. Teachers can help by providing a view for parents of their children's competence. Sharing children's work with parents is just as important at this age as in kindergarten.

When twelve-year-olds are offered reasonable responsibilities at school, most will respond with pride. Twelves make excellent one-on-one tutors for younger children. With help, they can manage a school store or recycling program, raise money and collect goods for needy families, or put out a class or school newspaper. Twelves can participate in student councils, organize their first school dance, or plan the spring field trip.

But smaller and more mundane responsibilities, such as keeping their room clean, may elude them. (This, by the way, is not the battle to pick with twelves.) At school, keeping track of things like assignments, books, papers, and sweatshirts isn't a priority. Excuses are constant and often transparent and humorous. The oldest homework excuse in the world—"My dog ate it"—is still put forth by twelve-year-olds. Along with other classics, such as "I couldn't find any paper in the house," "I left my book on the bus," and "You didn't tell us it was due today," teachers also now hear "The printer chewed up my paper, " "My dad was using the computer," and "My baby sister erased all my files." And on and on . . .

The twelve-year-old's ability to be totally responsible and totally irresponsible at the same time can be annoying, even infuriating, to adults. For the twelves, it is simply a matter of priorities. Teachers who hold class meetings and discussions of consequences will be more successful in getting twelves to accept responsibility for their behavior.

Twelves will have reasonable and unreasonable ideas for changing the way the classroom and the school operate. A dress code, chewing gum in school, or having a school dance can become major issues. Fairness and the process of making rules become more important. Twelves need opportunities to discuss and modify rules, but it's essential to keep rules consistent and to maintain ultimate adult authority clearly and calmly. Teachers must be fair and firm.

Physical energy drives twelve-year-olds. Both boys and girls are now in growth spurts, though puberty comes first to the girls. Both genders, however, require enormous amounts of sleep, food, and exercise. Schools don't commonly provide enough time for either food or exercise, yet twelves will thrive in a classroom where food is allowed. A midmorning snack is just as essential to a twelve-year-old's growing body as to a five-year-old's. A five-minute run around the building or a ten-minute game on the playground can rejuvenate the oxygen-hungry brain of an older child as well as that of a younger one.

Physical exercise not only helps twelves do better academically, but in the form of team sports, it can also provide some of the rites of passage twelves need as they enter the teen years. For those not athletically inclined, participating in groups and activities such as

computer and chess clubs, service organizations, Junior Achievement, and scouting can help build bridges into adult-like roles and participation in society.

Rituals and ceremonies can be deeply meaningful to twelve-year-olds as part of their rites of passage. Confirmation and bat or bar mitzvah ceremonies have profound meaning, and many children prepare for these events seriously, with a sense of importance and purpose. Schools can provide similar ceremonial experiences through graduations, honor assemblies, and service and athletic awards. Twelves and young teens need tangible recognition (from adults as well as peers) that they are changing and growing into responsible members of the adult community.

Twelve-Year-Olds: Growth Patterns

PHYSICAL

- Very energetic; need lots of sleep, exercise, and food (including in-school snacks)

- Enjoy physical education and sports

- Boys and girls both have growth spurts

- Girls show signs of puberty; most are menstruating

SOCIAL-EMOTIONAL

- Adult personality begins to emerge

- Capable of self-awareness, insight, and empathy; more reasonable and tolerant than at eleven

- Enthusiastic and uninhibited; appear to feel secure

- Care more about peer opinions than those of teachers and parents

- Will initiate their own activities without adult prompting

- Understand and enjoy sarcasm, double meanings, word play, and more sophisticated jokes

- Enjoy conversation with adults and peers

- Value peer vocabulary (slang)

- More able to think abstractly

- May begin to excel at a subject (such as science) or a skill (such as drawing)

- Can and will see both sides of an argument

- Very interested in civics, history, current events, politics, social justice, and environmental issues, as well as pop culture and the latest cool clothes, watches, etc.

- Increasingly able to organize their thoughts and their work

Twelve-Year-Olds in the Classroom

VISION AND FINE MOTOR ABILITY	▪ Increased fine motor ability, patience for practice, and self-confidence make all fine motor tasks more pleasurable
	▪ With better visual concentration, will read for long periods and spend more time on the computer learning word processing and other skills
	▪ Still enjoy handwork; interested in more complicated visual-motor tasks such as carpentry, mechanical repair, clothing design, and architecture
GROSS MOTOR ABILITY	▪ Many find team sports satisfying; also enjoy individual work in dance, drama, martial arts, and gymnastics
	▪ Understand the idea of training and regular exercise as a means to improve physical ability
	▪ Enjoy teaching physical skills to younger children
COGNITIVE GROWTH	▪ Find current events, civics, and history highly motivating when tied to issues of clear relevance to their lives
	▪ More interested, and at greater depth, in drama, debate, and performance; increasingly understand and appreciate the need for rehearsal and revision (true in writing also)
	▪ With their growing ability to set realistic short-term goals, more able to handle lengthy homework assignments due over longer periods, though these can be

continued on next page

problematic if they extend over weekends; planning
and organization of assignments improves

- Can help peers significantly with schoolwork; will
make good use of time allowed for peer conferencing,
partner projects, working as science lab partners, etc.

- Both playful and serious—love to play class games
but can have a serious discussion a moment later

- Can better integrate their learning when schools use
collaborative, cross-disciplinary teaching models and
self-contained classrooms (as opposed to isolated
subject matter and distinct class periods)

- Leadership qualities abound; need many opportunities for activities such as cross-age tutoring, jobs
at school, community service, hosting visitors, and
providing child care during parent meetings

- Appreciate teachers who listen and respond to their
suggestions for changes in routines, when realistic

- Benefit immensely from (and want to help plan)
ceremonies and rituals to mark turning points on
their way to adulthood

- Need access to significant adults, other than teachers
and parents, who will listen to them and help them
think about serious issues such as drugs, alcohol, sex,
AIDS, violence, and family problems

- Want to make money from jobs at home or in their
neighborhood

Twelve-Year-Olds: Curriculum

READING

Provide opportunities for children this age to:

- Continue reading trade books

- Begin reading newspapers and magazines for current events information, working with charts and graphs, and using books and other written sources for scientific information

- Read trilogies and book series; favorite topics include history, sports, science fiction, and fiction with themes tied to current events and social justice

- Recognize and discuss formal aspects of fiction— setting, character, etc.

- Complete research reports based on readings from several sources

- Learn library skills: work with an atlas, do computer searches, etc.

WRITING

Expect from these children:

- *Writing:* Increased facility with revision, particularly when changes result from peer conferences; interest in writing biographies and autobiographies, brief essays about world concerns such as racism, poverty, and environmental issues, and pieces linked to reading-program genres such as diaries, fantasies, and myths; interest in working on class or school newspaper

- *Spelling:* Functional for most; spell checkers and other computer interventions help those continuing to have trouble

continued on next page

- *Writing Themes:* Summarizing and writing briefly and clearly about teen issues (sex, drugs, music, cars); emotional poetry; "editorial" writing full of extreme positions; use of vernacular or slang in fiction; interesting dialogue

- *Handwriting:* Functional cursive for most; all are ready to use the computer to write; pleasure in practicing handwriting by writing letters, invitations, and thank-you notes; some interest in calligraphy

Favorite themes for children this age:

- Politics (including student politics)

- Current events

- Community service projects

- Fundraising (as a theme to be studied)

- History

- Racism

- Elementary economics and statistics

- Computer simulations

- Scientific experimentation and the microscopic world

Provide opportunities for children this age to:

- Begin pre-algebra studies through extensive work with unknowns

- Use math as tool for understanding science

- Compute extensively with decimals, fractions, and percents

- Solve geometric problems

Thirteen-Year-Olds

*"Today I am a teenager. I don't know what
I'm feeling right now."*

The Diary of Latoya Hunter: My First Year in Junior High

by Latoya Hunter

Thirteen is an age of dramatic contrasts. Because thirteen-year-olds commonly slip backward in their development as well as moving forward, on one day they may seem like younger twelve-year-olds, and on another day, more grown up than they really are. They may be excited one minute and bored the next, suddenly confident and just as suddenly withdrawn or even frightened. "Leave me alone!" is almost a mantra, yet they do not want to be alone for long. A day of depression, when no one likes them and they do not like themselves, when they hole up in their room and brood alone, may be followed by a day of giddiness, of shrieking and shouting with friends, the door to their room closed, the music turned up, energy erupting into roughhousing and pillow fights. Life at thirteen seems very confusing, and thirteen-year-olds can seem very confusing to their parents and teachers.

Boredom is a mask worn by thirteen-year-olds. At this age, "bored" translates as "insulted." Rather than the "scared/bored" of eight-year-olds, this is the "challenging/bored" of adolescents desperately seeking an identity and wanting grownups to simultaneously notice them, to see them as capable young people, and to leave them alone. Students at this age who complain that their teachers are boring are often expressing their perception that teachers are not acknowledging them as important individuals in the classroom. At the same time, a teacher's recognition can produce extreme embarrassment—the feeling of being put on the spot.

Thirteen-year-olds are excited about the possibilities of the teenage years, about new freedoms and informal rites of passage—going to the mall *just* with their friends; hanging out; having more control over telephone and computer time; being in a school with higher grade levels, often with or near the high schoolers; and studying harder subjects. For girls, being thirteen is directly connected to both excitement and apprehension about physical changes and their own developing sexuality. By thirteen, most girls have begun menstruating and are experiencing all the physical changes of adolescence. Thirteen-year-old girls are famous for spending hours in front of the mirror.

Boys at this age, on the other hand, are just beginning to experience signs of puberty. Growth of body hair, genital changes, nocturnal emissions, and other signs of male adolescence emerge as early as eleven in some, but most boys will not experience all of these changes until they are at least fourteen or fifteen. Nowhere on the developmental continuum is there greater physical and emotional separation between human beings of the same age than between girls and boys at thirteen.

For thirteens, THE ROOM at home is the defining space. Through their bedrooms (or spaces in a shared bedroom), teenagers say to their families, "I am here, but I am separate," "I am here, but look who I am now!" Through decorating and redecorating their rooms or room spaces, teenagers show what they identify with and who

they are. The powerful photo essay book *In My Room: Teenagers in Their Bedrooms* (Salinger 1995) meaningfully documents the changing icons of adolescence. My daughter, now in her thirties, remembers the progression of her own room's icons and decor: Michael Jackson (ages 8–10); Bon Jovi (ages 11–13); pink walls, a burgundy rug, and the Beatles, Marilyn Monroe, and "hunk" men on the walls (ages 14–15); a tapestry on the ceiling, white walls decorated with painted collages, written quotes, and pictures of friends (age 16); black walls, constellations on the walls and ceiling (astronomy and physics, not depression—she swears) at age 17.

When parents give over the bedroom, however, it does not mean giving up the child or giving away parental authority. But it does mean that both parent and child must recognize that along with the increased freedom for the child comes increased responsibility. Thus, parents may stop requiring that bedrooms be kept clean and neat by their child, but they should also then stop picking up laundry *for* their child. If the room is off limits, then the responsibility for the contents of the room ought also to be off limits. For the thirteen-year-old, learning to balance freedom and responsibility is a key developmental struggle in the creation of a healthy identity.

Although the room offers a safe haven for thirteens, a parent must also be unafraid to knock and walk in—or ask when a good time to come in might be, thereby shifting the locus of control ever so slightly, but not relinquishing parental authority. Most thirteen-year-olds desperately want to talk with their parents, but they do not know how to start the conversation. They need their parents to make the first move. The trouble is, although most parents of thirteen-year-olds also desperately want to talk with their teenagers, they too often do not know how to begin.

I suggest that parents say little and listen a lot. One of the most important of parenting (and teaching) skills, listening is of great value for connecting with thirteen-year-olds. I have found two books by Adele Faber and Elaine Mazlish immensely helpful in thinking about how to start and continue meaningful dialogue with all children. The first book is *How to Talk So Kids Will Listen & Listen So Kids Will Talk* (Faber and Mazlish 1980); the second is *How to Talk So Kids Can Learn at Home and in School* (Faber and Mazlish 1995).

School as well as home presents many challenges to the thirteen-year-old. When it comes to schoolwork, thirteens can often be withdrawn and sensitive, tentative and hesitant. They desperately need supportive teachers who gently encourage risk-taking in the classroom.

Socially, in contrast to the insular protection of their rooms at home, school for most thirteen-year-olds is a rotating series of classrooms, teachers, and groups of peers. Chris Stevenson, in his excellent book *Teaching Ten to Fourteen Year Olds*, has this to say about teenagers in school:

> There's no question that they are crying out to be together in settings where they are accepted and enjoyed by others [emphasis added]. Meanwhile, the organization of large, impersonal schools works against this need by imposing schedules that have students changing classes and classmates every thirty or forty minutes. An eighth grader who felt alienated from her school because the way it was organized kept her separated from many of her friends said cynically, "I think they're just trying to keep us away from each other so we'll stay confused." (Stevenson 1992, 106)

Although many middle and junior high schools have used block scheduling and teaming, which allow students to have more social interaction, these schools remain in the minority, and many are moving back to standard subject periods of forty-five to fifty-five minutes. Yet, it has been documented across cultures that cognitive development is greatly enhanced through social interaction. American schools emphasize individual achievement, yet we learn best when we are with others. Cognitive growth is enhanced in environments that foster and respect social interaction—where learners are accepted and enjoyed by others (Rogoff 1990).

Whether their school uses block scheduling or conventional forty-five to fifty-five minute periods, out-of-school activities are especially important for thirteen-year-olds. At thirteen the propensity to hibernate, avoid, keep to oneself, stay in one's room, and stay on the telephone or computer needs to be countered by opportunities to step out into the world of school sports, dances, student governance, community service, and other structured activities, as well as opportunities to enjoy unstructured but monitored peer group time. Through these experiences, thirteens develop the cognitive, social-emotional, and moral strength they will need for the years ahead.

Thirteen-Year-Olds: Growth Patterns

PHYSICAL

- Lots of physical energy

- Skin problems are common; hygiene becomes more important

- Most girls are menstruating and have reached almost full physical development

- Most boys are showing first signs of puberty (they will reach full development at fourteen or fifteen) and are physically awkward

SOCIAL-EMOTIONAL

- Very concerned about personal appearance, but unconcerned about the neatness of their personal environment (rooms at home, lockers or desks at school)

- Often quieter than twelves or fourteens

- Like to be left alone when at home

- Moody and sensitive; anger can flare up suddenly

- Their feelings are easily hurt, and they can easily hurt others' feelings; frequent meanness may stem from being insecure or scared

- Girls tend to focus on close friendships; boys tend to travel in small groups or gangs

- Spend hours on the computer or playing video games

continued on next page

- Feel and exert a lot of peer pressure concerning what to wear, how to talk, what music to listen to, etc.

- Boys still engage in a lot of horseplay and practical jokes

- Both girls and boys show a strong interest in sports

- Worry about schoolwork

- Increasingly punctuate their humor with sarcasm

- Enjoy collecting things (jewelry, make-up, music, movies)

- Want to know and use current peer language

- Answer parents with a single word or loud, extreme language

- Some beginning to be more capable of abstract reasoning

- Tentative, worried, and unwilling to take risks on tough intellectual tasks

- Like to challenge intellectual as well as social authority

Thirteen-Year-Olds in the Classroom

MOTOR ABILITY	■ Boys move awkwardly; girls are more agile
	■ Upper body strength lacking in both boys and girls
	■ May get headaches and feel fatigued from too much close eye work
COGNITIVE GROWTH	■ Interested in man's inhumanity to man and issues of fairness and justice; want to serve others
	■ Likes and dislikes become more pronounced (for example, may love math and hate English, or vice versa)
	■ May be afraid of journal writing, through which they might reveal too much; or, at the opposite extreme, may pour out their needs to a teacher or friend
	■ Can enjoy reading and writing about subjects that interest them; tend to dislike grammar and spelling
	■ Often write better than they speak and are therefore better at written work than oral explanations
	■ Need short, regular, predictable homework assignments to build good study habits
	■ Benefit from opportunities to balance teacher evaluation and grading with self-evaluation of their schoolwork
	■ Begin to enjoy thinking about the many sides of an issue or solutions to a problem

- Will not do as well in cooperative groups as twelves or older teens—tend to argue or complain about fairness; prefer solitary activity or working with a single partner on a project

- Will challenge teachers, asking, "Why do we have to learn this?"

- Highly judgmental of teachers, either positively or negatively, and like to discuss opinions about teachers with other students

- Bus behavior can be very problematic or out of control, especially for boys

- Gym (including dressing and showering), health, and sex education classes often embarrass them and lead to silly or rude behavior

- Can think globally, but often can't act locally; for example, concerned about social justice issues, but often mean to each other

Thirteen-Year-Olds: Curriculum

READING

Provide opportunities for children this age to:

- Read fiction and nonfiction involving social issues

- Extensively study literary elements—plot, character, mood, setting, and theme

- Read aloud as a class; use sources dealing with social topics such as conformity, crime, and homelessness as springboards to discussion and better understanding

- Acquire vocabulary from context as well as the dictionary and thesaurus

- Use textual references to document their statements

WRITING

Expect from these children:

- *Writing:* Ability to revise with careful attention to the difference between critique and personal criticism; pride in using proper writing mechanics; beginning ability to structure short expository essays with a thesis statement and supporting details; ability to summarize

- *Spelling:* Functional for most (those with ongoing spelling difficulty appreciate handheld spell checkers)

- *Writing Themes:* Writing that springs from topics in curricular literature; stories about social peer issues that focus on justice versus injustice, and inclusion versus exclusion

- *Handwriting:* Functional cursive for most (computers help those still having difficulty and are valuable for all students, particularly to ease the task of revising)

Favorite themes for children this age:

- Issues of resource use that are visible in students' lives, such as waste generation, disposal, and recycling; energy generation and use; and hunger and the growth, distribution, and consumption of food

- Historical conflicts (such as pro-slavery forces vs. abolitionists in the United States, the clash of Native American and European cultures, and the American Revolution), with reflection on their resolution and impact on various aspects of people's lives

- Historical biographies

- Study of the building blocks of the physical world, including water, air, and soil

MATH

Provide opportunities for children this age to:

- Review all operations, with special emphasis on conversion of decimals, fractions, and percents

- Make mathematical sets and do attribute mapping; study number patterns; explore the Fibonacci, binary, geometric, and other number sequences

- Extensively use geometric tools such as the compass and straightedge in sophisticated ways to construct and organize space

- Develop a thirty-word geometric vocabulary

- Engage in mathematical conversations about the concept of zero and negative numbers

- Begin learning algebra

Fourteen-Year-Olds

"I'm kind of small for fourteen even though I have a good build,
and those guys were bigger than me."

The Outsiders | *by S. E. Hinton*

———

Now it's time for the boys to join the girls in spending hours in front of the mirror. Aware of their physical changes and increasingly aware of the girls around them, many fourteen-year-old boys are entering puberty. Most of the girls are already there. Along with a shared awareness of their own and each other's physical selves, both genders at fourteen also share a need to distance themselves from adults as they do the all-important work of this age: beginning to forge a sense of self and a group identity.

In adolescence, the developing person begins to focus on the "Who am I?" question that is so central to human existence. As noted in 1968 by Erik Erikson, the developmental psychologist whose work remains the primary source for understanding social and emotional growth in Western culture, adolescents often seem "preoccupied with what they appear to be in the eyes of others as compared with what they feel they are" (Erikson 1968, 128). To the fourteen-year-old, questions about "who I am" seem best answered in terms of "who we are." Both boys and girls put enormous physical, emotional, and cognitive energy into the development of an adolescent subculture. At home, bedroom decor advertises to the family the image they are trying on. Out in the world, clothes, hairstyle, music, and

167

language—portable aspects of self—advertise fourteens' understanding of what is "cool" in the teen subculture. Traveling with teens as they move around in school, on the street, or at the mall, these portable image advertisements serve the all-important function of attracting other teens—while tending to put off adults.

This movement toward peers and away from parents and teachers as the central figures in their lives is a key step in the distancing dance of young adolescents. When I asked thirteen- and fourteen-year-olds to whom they would turn for advice about a serious problem, both ages mentioned their parents, but the fourteen-year-olds said they would also consult their best friends. Distancing from adults is also expressed by the awkward embarrassment at this age of being seen with parents, of having parents wear uncool clothes, drive an old car, or say the wrong thing. Eye-rolling, hair tossing, and scornful facial expressions are some of the distancing gestures parent can expect to see from fourteen-year-olds.

Challenging the authority of the adult now becomes almost a visceral reaction. Teens this age often seem to argue for arguing's sake. Fourteen-year-olds want to do it their way, to have freedom, to be on their own. They're looking constantly for opportunities to decide for themselves what they will do—such as get a part-time job, play a sport, join a rock band—"and at the same time are mortally afraid of being forced into activities in which they would feel exposed to ridicule or self-doubt" (Erikson 1968, 129). Such embarrassing activities might include going out to eat with parents or dressing up.

This typically teen behavior, which often peaks at fifteen, has to do with what Erikson calls the struggle of each adolescent: the search for "fidelity." By fidelity he means a strong loyalty or devotion to an emerging sense of self, to some other person or persons, to ideas or fads. Fourteen-year-olds can exhibit this intense devotion to a sport or a musical instrument, to body piercing, or to a friendship or an idol. All of this practice around issues of fidelity helps prepare

adolescents to participate as devoted, disciplined, loving partners and full-fledged citizens when they become adults.

Successful development of fidelity depends substantially on the guidelines, customs, and rites of passage provided by family, heritage, and society at large. Yet American society offers relatively few rites of passage for fourteen-year-olds. To fill the void, some families are creating "passage parties" that honor the adolescent's dawning adulthood. Other families find safe, structured, ways to offer their physically active teens solo hikes, high ropes courses, etc. All such passage experiences help adolescents think about and practice disciplined and constructive devotion to oneself and others.

Still, despite the importance of family, camps, church, and other social arenas, society for the fourteen-year-old is primarily school. School is the main structured social setting where society makes its demands on the adolescent. How the school is structured and how it places demands on students are critically important factors in the development of healthy young adults for our future society.

Take the demand for doing homework. Many fourteen-year-olds say they wish they didn't have homework. They resent it and don't see the point of it, except that if they don't do it, it lowers their grades and might mean detention and missing after-school activities. But if adults understand fourteen-year-olds' need to challenge homework and respond in a spirit of negotiation, then fourteen-year-olds will more likely be disciplined in doing it. If, however, homework is meted out as menial work or punishment, fourteen-year-olds will resist and rebel.

One positive way to deal with homework for a rebellious teen is for the teacher and student to discuss the amount of homework the student can accomplish on a given night. Thus, the student will not be assigned the same amount as other students each night, but will be challenging himself to do his personal best. A student who is ready for three math problems one night will be given three problems, with the teacher helping her to understand that the next night the minimum will be four and so on. This "incremental success" approach to homework respects individual differences and needs, yet also respects high standards by increasing accountability inch by inch.

Such an approach to homework is one example of how adults can help make adolescence a building ground instead of a battleground. This adult willingness to negotiate can also be helpful in regard to adolescents' response to in-school assignments, after-school activities, and chores at home. Each encounter offers the adolescent apprenticeship in adulthood through respectful interaction with caring adults.

Both at home and in school, the more we create positive demands, rites of passages, and traditions that let us take the time to truly listen to fourteen-year-olds, the more likely it is that fidelity will emerge. Listening to our fourteen-year-olds is not the same as giving in to their demands. Listening means confirming their experience, acknowledging their presence, and accepting and enjoying them.

At school, this means setting aside more time for counseling, peer tutoring, community service, and advisories (small groups of students talking regularly with each other and the same teacher about school and life). We need to stop seeing these elements as add-on's to an outmoded, rigid system of subject matter accountability and start seeing them as the proper structures for healthy and productive adolescent growth and development.

Our traditional model of schooling for young adolescents assumes that a miniature high school or college environment will get the students ready for life as adults. What this model misses is that adolescents cannot get ready for the future by living in it. Instead, adolescents must be given an environment in which they can work through the issues of fidelity. It is the structures we create, not the struggles of youth, that are responsible for the future. Adults must take responsibility to look through new eyes at the way we structure adolescents' school day, how we teach them, and how we relate to them.

At home, this investment of time is equally critical. Despite the fact that fourteen-year-olds want to spend all their time on the phone, at the mall, or with their friends, we must not give away our adult responsibility to set aside family time for listening and discussion on a regular, structured schedule. We also must not be intimidated by the threats and tears of our teenagers when we do so. It is hard, but we must be the adults. "Family Meetings" are one popular format for allowing discussion and decision making by all family members (Nelsen 2006). More informal listening time—the knock on the door of the sacred bedroom—is also important. And try to resist the temptation to talk with your teenager when anger is in the air. This is not the time to exert your adult power; instead exercise your adult restraint and set up a time to talk later when you are both cooled down. By our example, we provide guidance even as our children seem to push us away.

Often, as fourteen turns into fifteen, a seemingly greater gulf opens between parent and teenager, teacher and adolescent student. The following letter is a real-life example:

> *Dear Mom and Dad,*
>
> *The reason I'm writing this letter is simply because spoken words do NOT seem to get through; I try to talk to you and sometimes you listen but other times …*
>
> *You say that you're the adult and that you're in control but part of being in control is being able to listen to other people and be willing to make some changes.*
>
> *I'm not a little girl and to be honest I don't even consider myself a "child" anymore. Maybe by my birthdate I'm not old enough to make important decisions about MY life. But looking at my maturity and intelligence levels, I think it's about time you let me be in control of my life.*
>
> *It seems like you guys have this thing with power. Like having power and control over my life is your ultimate goal.*
>
> *If you don't let me go now, when you finally do, I won't come back. You're showering me with too many limits and too much of your protective "love." You're both driving me away.*

If this is how it's going to be until I turn 21 or even 16 I don't want to be a part of it or a part of your lives. I love you mom and dad, but I'm sick of the way I'm being treated. Don't my feelings count too?

I've been thinking a lot about "running away." And if that's the only way I can get through to you, I will do it!! There are plenty of places that I can go. This is not a threat so you will say, "okay, do whatever you want." These are the facts, the way things are going to be until you let me go to live my own life. It's your choice.

MY life and well-being are as important to me as they are to you. Let ME be in control. It's MY life.

> *"Some men see things as they are and say why,*
> *I dream things that never were and say why not"*

—your daughter

Sometimes it is hard to empathize with adolescents. But we need to understand that emotions such as those expressed by this fifteen-year-old are both a pushing away and a deep desire to remain connected, all a part of the struggle to learn fidelity. Fidelity—to parents and teachers—can certainly reemerge as one of the blessings of our relationships with our older adolescents.

Fourteen-Year-Olds: Growth Patterns

PHYSICAL

- Very energetic, generally healthy; because being with peers is so important, most would rather go to school than stay home when they're sick

- Need lots of exercise, snacks, and sleep

- Girls are almost fully developed

- Growth spurts continue for boys, and their upper body strength begins to develop

- Both genders are more interested in sex; some are sexually active

SOCIAL-EMOTIONAL

- Crave adult connection even while fighting for their own identity; need adults to listen and negotiate rules and requirements

- Often embarrassed to be seen with their parents; fiercely critical of parents' dress, habits, friends, and ideas

- Adult personality continues to develop

- Like to cram as much into each day as they possibly can

- Typically loud and rambunctious

- Are in a "know it all" stage, in which they especially dislike and respond poorly to adult lectures, feeling they know what will be said once they hear the first few words

continued on next page

- Safe, positive rites of passage can be important to emerging sense of self

- Can be a pain at home and a star at school

- Very concerned with using the slang that is popular with their peers but also want to learn how to communicate in the adult world

- Will engage more in group discussion

- Interested in word meanings and in developing a broader vocabulary

- Better at figuring out cause and effect and doing other abstract thinking

- More willing to admit an error and try something a second or third time

- Very aware of problems in the larger world and generally still invested in learning more and finding solutions

- Like technology and learning how things work

Fourteen-Year-Olds in the Classroom

MOTOR ABILITY	▪ Need as much physical release as possible through brief periods outdoors, a run around the playground, or a stretch break in the classroom
	▪ Find it difficult to maintain "good" posture and sit "properly" in typical school furniture; they do well when allowed to lounge or sprawl on the floor for part of their class time
	▪ If given time for a rest period, quiet reading, or a nap, they often perform and behave better in the afternoon
COGNITIVE GROWTH	▪ Respond well to academic variety and challenge
	▪ Learn well in small discussion groups (eight to ten students) or cooperative learning groups (fewer than eight students)
	▪ Enjoy and do well with lengthier project assignments
	▪ Intrigued by research and putting together research reports in the proper format
	▪ Many show increased interest in math and science
	▪ Enjoy talking about current events formally in class or informally with their peers
	▪ Take pleasure in developing individual skills (for example, music, art, or handwork) that express their particular emerging adult intelligence
	▪ Often say "I'm bored" to mean "I don't understand"

continued on next page

- Like having a chance to evaluate and improve their own work and can also constructively critique other students' work

- Complain about homework, but often enjoy the challenge

- Often say work is too easy when they find it plenty challenging

- Interested in studying psychology as a means of answering the "Who am I?" question

- May give in to peer pressure to see doing well in school as "nerdy" and "uncool"

- Service projects, student government, class dances, sporting events, and other group undertakings often lead to a first career interest

- Begin to develop distinctive sense of humor; can be extremely funny and creative

- Usually loud; balance in classroom expectations is important (that is, requiring silence sometimes, but not always)

Fourteen-Year-Olds: Curriculum

Provide opportunities for children this age to:

- Use literary themes to support their intensifying quest for identity and exploration of perspectives on the self and others

- Sample many genres, such as song lyrics, poetry, drama, short story, and novel

- Study how literary elements interweave—for example, how characterization can forward the plot of a story

- Express their understanding of the difference between fact and opinion

- Use textual references in writing and discussion

- Use language as tool for different purposes (for example, to tell a story versus advertise a product)

- Participate in class read-alouds, which they continue to find an appealing springboard for discussion

- Continue their increasingly sophisticated vocabulary study; for some, begin work with the logic of analogies

Expect from these children:

- *Writing:* Interest in choosing appropriate genre (poem, play, story) in which to represent their ideas; experimentation with different voices, often tied in with literature they're studying; writing from different points of view; more deliberate use of grammatical constructions for

continued on next page

stylistic reasons; beginning use of conventional footnotes, endnotes, and bibliographic entries

- *Spelling:* Functional for most; use of spell checkers when writing on computers; use of handheld spell checkers for those with ongoing spelling difficulties

- *Writing Themes:* Motivation to write in preparation for activities such as debates and mock trials, which increasingly require them to structure and defend their thinking; use of literary themes as a springboard for writing assignments and creative writing; ability to do longer research papers related to thematic studies; willingness to write journals with adults (teens and adults respond to each other's entries) as a means of sorting out issues in their own lives and the larger world

- *Handwriting:* Increasing fluency with computers as assignments become longer and more complex

Favorite themes for children this age:

- Physical and human geography

- Current world conflicts, with emphasis upon causes and possible resolutions

- Facts about natural resources and how current lifestyles affect them; for example, the impact of development on plants, animals, and indigenous peoples of the rain forest

- Basic physical and biological principles, such as the power of the crowbar, the dynamics of flight, and osmosis and the transport of water in trees

continued on next page

Fourteen-Year-Olds: Curriculum

MATH

Provide opportunities for children this age to:

- Review all operations with special emphasis on ratio and proportion

- Read and use graphs, particularly circle and bar graphs

- Explore number systems with numbers other than 10 as their base

- Work with the binary number system (which uses only the digits 0 and 1)

- Solve equations with a single unknown

- Explore how functions describe the interaction of two variables

- Study formal algebra

Acknowledgments

———

This book would never have been written without my close association with many wonderful professionals at Gesell Institute of Child Development, where I was first trained in developmental observation and later became a certified trainer. I am especially grateful to Jackie Haines and to the late Dr. Louise Bates Ames, with whom I spent many hours discussing the history of the Child Development Movement in America as well as the details of individual children's behavior (including that of my own son and daughter).

Marlynn K. Clayton and Deborah Porter taught my children and taught with me in two schools during our careers. We learned much together, and I am grateful for all they did to support me as a young principal and my wife and me as parents many years ago.

Thanks to other colleagues and co-founders at Northeast Foundation for Children and Greenfield Center School: Gretchen Bukowick, co-founder Ruth Sidney Charney, Paula Denton, the late Marion Finer, Mary Beth Forton, co-founder Jay Lord, and especially Roxann Kriete, the current executive director at NEFC. Together, we shared for over twenty years—and continue to share—our own developmental pathways as educators. [Publisher's note: Northeast Foundation for Children is the former name of Center for Responsive Schools.]

Thanks also to everyone who has taught me so much over the past four years about shared learning and leadership at Sheffield Elementary School and in the Gill-Montague Regional School District.

Deep appreciation to all in the Courage to Teach movement with whom I have kept company the last ten years in reflective listening and learning, especially Pamela Seigle, Lisa Sankowski, Rick and Marcy Jackson, and Parker Palmer.

Over my nearly forty years in education and child development, I have been blessed to come in contact and work with so many other extraordinary people who have continued to help frame my thinking about the important issues in this book. There are really too many to name and I would surely leave someone out, but I know in my heart that you know who you are.

I am indebted to the contribution of assistant professor Iliana Reyes at the University of Arizona for taking the time to consult with me on the cultural and linguistic diversity section of the book. Her ongoing research will be of great value to the field of child development and to the national debate on biliteracy.

Special thanks to NEFC editor Elizabeth Nash for her graciousness, patience, and helpfulness in the process of preparing this revision; to Alice Yang, NEFC publications manager, for enduring optimism about this project; and to readers Fay Brown, Marlynn Clayton, Paula Denton, Iliana Reyes, and Amy Wade, who took the time to consider the book in its entirety toward the end of the project.

Finally to my family . . . my beloved wife, Irene Laurent Wood; my children, Jonathan Laurent-Wood and Heather Heaton; my grandchildren and new instructors in child development, Isaiah Robert Heaton and Lily Aliyah Heaton; my son-in-law Joel Heaton; and my sister Claudia Rahm and her family, for all the love and tending.

References

American Association for the Child's Right to Play. www.ipausa.org/recess_advocates_list.htm.

Ames, L. B. 1989. *Arnold Gesell: Themes of His Work.* New York: Human Sciences Press.

Ashton-Warner, S. 1963. *Teacher.* New York: Simon & Schuster.

Baker, C., and S. P. Jones, Eds. 1998. *Encyclopedia of Bilingualism and Bilingual Education.* Clevedon, United Kingdom: Multilingual Matters.

Bradley, C. 2005. "Multiple-Lens Paradigm Evaluating African American Girls and Their Development: Practice & Theory." *Journal of Counseling and Development* (June).

Bransford, J. D., A. L. Brown, and R. R. Cocking. 1999. *How People Learn: Brain, Mind, Experience, and School.* Washington, D.C.: National Academy Press.

Brisk, M. E., and M. M. Harrington. 1999. *Literacy and Bilingualism: A Handbook for ALL Teachers.* Mahwah, New Jersey: Lawrence Erlbaum.

Bus, A. G., and M. H. van Ijzendoorn. 1988. "Mother-Child Interactions, Attachment and Emergent Literacy: A Cross-Sectional Study." *Child Development* 59: 1262–1272.

Cleary, B. 1968. *Ramona the Pest*. New York: William Morrow.

Cohen, M. 1980/2006. *First Grade Takes a Test*. Reprint, New York: Star Bright Books.

Collins, B. 1995. *The Art of Drowning*. Pittsburgh, Pennsylvania: University of Pittsburgh Press.

Comer, J. P., and A. F. Poussaint. 1992. *Raising Black Children: Two Leading Psychiatrists Confront the Educational, Social and Emotional Problems Facing Black Children*. New York: Plume.

Cummins, J. 2001. *Language, Power, & Ideology*. Bilingual Education & Bilingualism Series. Clevedon, UK: Multilingual Matters.

Dahl, R. 1975. *Danny, the Champion of the World*. New York: Knopf.

DeClements, B. 1981. *Nothing's Fair in Fifth Grade*. New York: Viking.

Delgado-Gaitán, C. 1992. "School Matters in the Mexican-American Home: Socializing Children to Education." *American Educational Research Journal* 29(3): 495–513.

Dillard, A. 1987. *An American Childhood*. New York: Harper & Row.

Dyson, A. H. 1983. "The Role of Oral Language in Early Writing." *Research in the Teaching of English* 17: 1–30.

Eisenberg, A. R. 2002. "Maternal Teaching Talk within Families of Mexican Descent: Influences of Task and Socioeconomic Status." *Hispanic Journal of Behavioral Sciences* 24: 206–24.

Elliot, D. C., and R. Capp. 2003. "The Gift of Time: Multi-Age Teaching and Curriculum Design, or Looping, to Provide a Curriculum That Maximizes Learning." *Leadership* (November/December).

Erikson, E. H. 1968. *Identity: Youth and Crisis.* New York: W.W. Norton.

Escamilla, K. 1987. "The Relationship of Native Language Reading Achievement and Oral English Proficiency to Future Achievement in Reading English As a Second Language." Unpublished doctoral dissertation. Univ. of California at Los Angeles.

Faber, A., and Mazlish, E. 1995. *How to Talk So Kids Can Learn at Home and in School.* New York: Simon & Schuster.

————. 1980. *How to Talk So Kids Will Listen & Listen So Kids Will Talk.* New York: Avon.

Ferreiro, E., and A. Teberosky. 1982. *Literacy before Schooling.* Exeter, New Hampshire: Heinemann.

Gilligan, C., N. P. Lyons, and T. J. Hammer, Eds. 1990. *Making Connections: The Relational Worlds of Adolescent Girls at the Emma Willard School.* Cambridge, Massachusetts: Harvard Univ. Press.

González, N., L. Moll, and R. Amanti. 2005. *Theorizing Home, School and Community Practices.* Mahwah, New Jersey: Lawrence Erlbaum.

Gordon, J. A. 2000. *The Color of Teaching.* New York: Routledge-Falmer.

Greene, B. *Phillip Hall Likes Me, I Reckon Maybe.* New York: Dial.

Gumperz, J. J., and N. Berenz. 1993. "Transcribing Conversational Exchanges." In *Talking Data.* J.A. Edwards and M.D. Lampert, Eds. Mahwah, New Jersey: Lawrence Erlbaum.

Hale-Benson, J. E. 2001. *Learning While Black: Creating Educational Excellence for African American Children.* Baltimore, Maryland: Johns Hopkins Univ. Press.

————. 1986. *Black Children: Their Roots, Culture, and Learning Styles.* Revised ed. Baltimore, Maryland: Johns Hopkins Univ. Press.

————. 1982. *Black Children: Their Roots, Culture, and Learning Styles.* Revised ed. Baltimore, Maryland: Johns Hopkins Univ. Press.

Hall, N., J. Larson, and J. Marsh. 2003. *Handbook of Early Childhood Literacy.* London: Sage.

Harste, J., V. Woodward, and C. Burke. 1984. *Language Stories and Literacy Lessons.* Portsmouth, New Hampshire: Heinemann.

Heath, S. B. 1983. *Ways with Words: Language, Life, and Work in Communities and Classrooms.* New York: Cambridge Univ. Press.

Holliday, B. G. 2001. "Foreword," *Forging Links: African American Children—Clinical Developmental Perspectives,* pp. xi–xii. Praeger Series in Applied Psychology. A. M. Neal-Barnett, J. M. Contreras, and K. A. Kerns, Eds. Westport, Connecticut: Praeger Publishers.

————. 1985. "Developmental Imperatives of Social Ecologies: Lessons Learned from Black Children." In *Black Children—Social, Educational, and Parental Environments,* pp. 53–69. 1st ed. H. P. McAdoo and J. L. McAdoo, Eds. Newbury Park, California: Sage.

Hinton, S. E. 1967. *The Outsiders.* New York: Viking Juvenile.

Hunter, L. 1992. *The Diary of Latoya Hunter: My First Year in Junior High.* New York: Crown.

Institute for Research on Poverty. Univ. of Wisconsin-Madison. www.irp.wisc.edu.

Kenner, C., G. Kress, A. Hayat, R. Kam, and K. Tsai. 2004. "Finding the Keys to Biliteracy: How Young Children Interpret Different Writing Systems." *Language and Education* 18(20): 124–144.

Konner, M. 1993. *Childhood: A Multicultural View.* New York: Little, Brown.

Lee, V. E., and D. Burkam. 2002. *Inequality at the Starting Gate.* Washington, D.C.: Economic Policy Institute.

Mason, J. A. 1980. "When Do Children Begin to Read: An Exploration of Four-Year-Old Children's Letter and Word Reading Competencies." *Reading Research Quarterly* 15: 203–225.

Mayo Clinic. 2007. "Dehydration: Signs and Symptoms." www .mayoclinic.com/health/dehydration/DS00561/DSECTION=2.

———. 2006. "Water: How Much Should You Drink Every Day?" www.mayoclinic.com/health/water/NU00283.

McAdoo, H. P., Ed. 2007. *Black Families.* Thousand Oaks, California: Sage.

———, Ed. 2002. *Black Children: Social, Educational, and Parental Environments.* Beverly Hills, California: Sage.

McAdoo, H. P. 2002. "The Village Talks: Racial Socialization of Our Children." In *Black Children: Social, Educational, and Parental Environments*, pp. 47–55, H. P. McAdoo, Ed. 2d ed. Thousand Oaks, California: Sage.

McAdoo, H. P., and J. L. McAdoo, Eds. 1985. *Black Children: Social, Educational, and Parental Environments.* Beverly Hills, California: Sage.

Miles, B. 1974. *The Real Me.* New York: Random House.

Milne, A. A. 1927. *Now We Are Six.* New York: E. P. Dutton & Co.

Moll, L. C. 1992. "Literacy Research in Community and Classrooms: A Sociocultural Approach." In *Multidisciplinary Perspectives in Literacy Research.* R. Beach, J. Green, M. Kamil, and T. Shanahan, Eds. Urbana, Illinois: National Conference on Research in English.

———. 1990. "Introduction," *Vygotsky and Education: Instructional Implications and Applications of Sociohistorical Psychology.* L. C. Moll, Ed. New York: Cambridge Univ. Press.

Montessori, M. 1909/1964. *The Montessori Method*. A. E. George, trans. Reprint, New York: Schocken.

Moreno, R. P. 1997. "Everyday Instruction: A comparison of Mexican American and Anglo Mothers and Their Preschool Children." *Hispanic Journal of Behavioral Sciences* 19: 527–539.

National Association for Year-Round Education. 2006. "Statistical Summaries of Year-Round Education Programs: 2005–2006." www.nayre.org, Calendar Reform Statistics, Statistical Summary 2006 (PDF format).

National Center for Children in Poverty. Columbia Univ. www.nccp.org.

National Education Association. 2003. "Status of the American Public School Teacher 2000–2001." Washington, D.C.: NEA Research.

National Sleep Foundation. 2000. "Adolescent Sleep Needs and Patterns: Research Report and Resource Guide." Washington, D.C.

Neal-Barnett, A. M., J. M. Contreras, and K. A. Kerns, Eds. 2001. *Forging Links: African American Children—Clinical Developmental Perspectives*. Praeger Series in Applied Psychology. Westport, Connecticut: Praeger.

Nelsen, J. *Positive Discipline*. 2d ed., updated. New York: Ballantine.

Nichols, G. W. 2002. "The Impact of Looping Classroom Environments on Parental Attitudes." *Preventing School Failure* (September 22).

Nottis, K. E. 2004. "Elementary Teachers' Beliefs and Knowledge about Grade Retention: How Do We Know What They Know?" *Education* (December 22).

Piaget, Jean. 1932/1965. *The Moral Judgment of the Child*. M. Gabain, trans. Reprint, New York: Free Press.

————. 1923/1959. *The Language and Thought of the Child.* M. Gabain, trans. Reprint, London: Routledge and Kegan Paul.

Pipher, M. 1994. *Reviving Ophelia: Saving the Selves of Adolescent Girls.* New York: Putnam.

Reese, L. 2002. "Parental strategies in contrasting cultural settings: Families in Mexico and 'El Norte'." *Anthropology & Education Quarterly* 33(1): 30–59.

Reese, L., and R. Gallimore. 2000. "Immigrant Latinos' Cultural Model of Literacy Development: An Evolving Perspective on Home-School Discontinuities." *American Journal of Education* 108(2): 103–134.

Reese, L., H. Garnier, R. Gallimore, and C. Goldenberg. 2000. "A Longitudinal Analysis of the Antecedents of Emergent Spanish Literacy and Middle-School English Reading Achievement of Spanish-Speaking Students." *American Educational Research Association Journal* 37: 633–662.

Reyes, I. 2006. "Exploring Connections between Emergent Biliteracy and Bilingualism." *Journal of Early Childhood Literacy* 6(3) 267–292.

————. 2004. "Functions of Code Switching in Schoolchildren's Conversations." *Bilingual Research Journal* 28(1): 77–98.

Reyes, I., D. Alexandra, and P. Azuara. 2006. "Home Literacy Practices in Mexican Households." Univ. of Arizona. Paper presented at the annual meeting of the American Educational Research Association, San Francisco (April 10).

Reyes, I., and L. Moll. 2005. "Latinos and Bilingualism." In *Encyclopedia Latina: History, Culture, and Society in the United States.* I. Stevens and H. Augenbraum, Eds. New York: Grolier Academic Reference.

Rivers, S. W., and F. Rivers. 2002. "Sankofa Shule Spells Success for African American Children." In *Black Children: Social, Educational, and Parental Environments*, p. 176. 2d ed. H. P. McAdoo, Ed. Thousand Oaks, California: Sage.

Rodriguez, G. G. 1999. *Raising Nuestros Niños: Bringing Up Latino Children in a Bicultural World*. New York: Fireside Books.

Rogoff, B. 2003. *The Cultural Nature of Human Development*. New York: Oxford Univ. Press.

———. 1990. *Apprenticeship in Thinking: Cognitive Development in Social Context*. New York: Oxford Univ. Press.

Romero, G. 1983. *"Print Awareness of the Pre-school Bilingual Spanish-English Speaking Child."* Unpublished doctoral dissertation. Univ. of Arizona, Tucson.

Salinger, A. 1995. *In My Room: Teenagers in Their Bedrooms*. San Francisco: Chronicle Books.

Stevenson, C. 1992. *Teaching Ten to Fourteen Year Olds*. White Plains, New York: Longman.

Street, B. 1997. "The Implications of the 'New Literacy Studies' for Literacy Education." *English in Education* 31(3): 45–59.

Sulzby, E., J. Barnhart, and J. Hiesima. 1990. "Forms of Writing and Rereading from Writing: A Preliminary Report." In *Reading and Writing Connections*, J. Mason, Ed. Needham Heights, Massachusetts: Allyn & Bacon.

Tabors, P., M. Paez, and L. Lopez. 2002. "Early Childhood Study of Language and Literacy Development of Spanish-Speaking Children: Theoretical Background and Preliminary Results." Paper presented at the annual meeting of the National Association of Bilingual Education, Pennsylvania.

Taylor, D. 1993. *From the Child's Point of View*. Portsmouth, New Hampshire: Heinemann.

Taylor, D., and C. Dorsey-Gaines. 1988. *Growing Up Literate*. Portsmouth, New Hampshire: Heinemann.

Teale, W. 1986. *The Beginnings of Reading and Writing: Written Language Development during the Preschool and Kindergarten Years*. In *The Pursuit Of Literacy: Early Reading and Writing*. M. Sampson, Ed. Dubuque, Iowa: Kendall/Hunt.

Teale, W., and E. Sulzby, Eds. 1986. *Emergent Literacy: Writing and Reading*. Norwood, New Jersey: Ablex.

Torres, J., J. Santos, N. L. Peck, and L. Cortes. 2004. *Minority Teacher Recruitment, Development, and Retention*. Providence, Rhode Island: Education Alliance at Brown Univ.

U.S. Department of Education, National Center for Education Statistics. 2006. "The Condition of Education 2006; Indicator 5: Racial/Ethnic Distribution of Public School Students." NCES 2006-071. Washington, D.C.: U.S. Government Printing Office.

———. 2003a. *Reading—Young Children's Achievement and Classroom Experience,* NCES 2003-070. Washington, D.C.: U.S. Government Printing Office. Quoted in I. Reyes, D. Alexandra, and P. Azuara, "Home Literacy Practices in Mexican Households," paper presented at the annual meeting of the American Educational Research Association, San Francisco, April 10, 2006, and used with permission of the authors.

———. 2003b. "Status and Trends in the Education of Hispanics." NCES 2003-008. Washington, D.C.: U.S. Government Printing Office.

———. 2002. "Digest of Education Statistics Tables and Figures," Table 101, "Selected characteristics of students, teachers, parent participation, and programs and services in traditional public and public charter elementary and secondary schools: 1999–2000." nces.ed.gov/programs/digest/d02/dt101.asp.

Valdés, G. 2003. *Expanding Definitions of Giftedness: The Case of Young Interpreters from Immigrant Communities.* Educational Psychology Series. New York: Teachers College Press.

———. 1996. *Con Respeto: Bridging the Distances Between Culturally Diverse Families and Schools.* New York: Teachers College Press.

Vásquez, O. A. 2003. *La Clase Mágica: Imagining Optimal Possibilities in a Bilingual Community of Learners.* Mahwah, New Jersey: Lawrence Erlbaum.

Vygotsky, L. 1934/1986. *Thought and Language.* A. Kozulin, trans. Reprint, Cambridge, Massachusetts: MIT Press.

White, E. B. 1952. *Charlotte's Web.* New York: Harper

Whitmore, K. F., P. Martens, Y. Goodman, and G. Owocki. 2004. "Critical Lessons From the Transactional Perspective on Early Literacy Research." *Journal of Early Childhood Literacy* 4(3): 291–325.

Williams, M. 1922. *The Velveteen Rabbit.* New York: Doubleday & Co.

Wood, C. 1999. *Time to Teach, Time to Learn: Changing the Pace of School.* Turners Falls, Massachusetts: Center for Responsive Schools, Inc.

Wood, D., and C. Fassnacht. 2005. *Transana Software.* Wisconsin Center for Education Research, Univ. of Wisconsin-Madison.

Zentella, A. C. 1997. *Growing Up Bilingual.* Malden, Massachusetts: Blackwell.

The Birthday Cluster Exercise

Where Is Your Class Developmentally?

———

Yardsticks contains lots of useful information about what children need at any given age in school. Yet a first question any teacher logically will have when reading the book is, "How do I apply this to a whole class of children? There is such a range of development in any class and every year my classes are so different."

The most practical way I know to apply the general developmental characteristics in the book is to use the birthday cluster exercise. Here's how to do it.

Create a Chronological Listing

As I have emphasized throughout the book, a child's chronological (or birthday age) and developmental age do not necessarily correlate directly, either physically, intellectually, emotionally, or socially. But, except for developmental screening in prekindergarten or kindergarten, teachers seldom have access to developmental data on the children in their classes, except in a case where there is concern about special needs a particular child may have. It is useful, therefore, to use children's chronological ages to get a sense of the developmental abilities and behaviors you're likely to see in a class.

A simple way to do this is to list the children in your class from youngest to oldest, using a "year, month" format to show each child's age (for example, 9 years, 2 months). From a complete list of children's ages, as shown in Figure 1, you can easily see the range of chronological ages you'll be teaching.

See Where the Birthdays Cluster

Once you've created your chronological list, you need to see where most birthdays cluster as of a given date—say on September 1. In our sample fourth grade chart (Figure 1), the greatest number of children are at 9 years, 7 months, on September 1st (five out of twenty-two), with another four at 9 years, 9 months, on the same date. So the birthday cluster in this classroom is in the 9 years, 7 to 9 months range. Creating a bar graph, as shown in Figure 2, can help you see the cluster.

Use What You've Learned

Once you've completed this exercise, you'll know whether the children you'll be teaching form a class that is, overall, young, old, or somewhere in between. In our sample fourth grade class, the cluster in the 9 years, 7 to 9 month range, plus the many children who are ten plus or minus a month, make it, overall, an old class.

What do you do now?

- Plan for a fourth grade class beginning the year with mostly older nine-year-old and ten-year-old developmental characteristics. Look back through the book at the classroom implications for these ages. Think about your room arrangement and about the curriculum activities that will most engage this class as a whole. Think about potential problem areas, especially socially, for the much younger children in the classroom as well as the older.

- Think about how the class will be different in the second half of the year, when many children (more than half by March) will

most likely be exhibiting ten-year-old developmental characteristics, with one or two possibly exhibiting eleven-year-old
characteristics. You'll need to adjust approaches to classroom
organization, instruction, classroom responsibilities, homework,
and many other areas by paying attention to children's shifting
development. Teachers who lose sight of the developmental
shifts within a given year may find themselves wondering why
they have more trouble with a class in the second half of the
year. Part of the solution may be paying more attention to how
teaching practices need to change to accommodate students'
changing developmental needs.

- Consider the potential needs of the children on the younger and
older ends of the spectrum. Think about how you will accommodate them as you see how they respond to daily classroom life.

Figure 1: Sample fourth grade chronological age chart, 2006–2007 school year

Name	Date of Birth	Chronological Age	
		9/1/06	3/1/07
Fernando	7/31/97	9 years, 1 month	9 years, 7 months
Austin	6/25/97	9 years, 2 months	9 years, 8 months
Justine	6/21/97	9 years, 2 months	9 years, 8 months
Shawana	6/12/97	9 years, 2 months	9 years, 8 months
Carolynne	2/6/97	9 years, 6 months	10 years, 0 months
Emma	1/14/97	9 years, 7 months	10 years, 1 month
Helena	1/27/97	9 years, 7 months	10 years, 1 month
Amario	1/26/97	9 years, 7 months	10 years, 1 month
Ginger	1/7/97	9 years, 7 months	10 years, 1 month
Martin	1/4/97	9 years, 7 months	10 years, 1 month
Ashleigh	11/30/96	9 years, 9 months	10 years, 3 months
Ben	11/29/96	9 years, 9 months	10 years, 3 months
Linda	11/18/96	9 years, 9 months	10 years, 3 months
Clemmie	11/4/96	9 years, 9 months	10 years, 3 months
Mack	10/18/96	9 years, 10 months	10 years, 4 months
Gawain	9/19/96	9 years, 11 months	10 years, 5 months

Name	Date of Birth	Chronological Age	
		9/1/06	3/1/07
Lupe	9/13/96	9 years, 11 months	10 years, 5 months
Bonnie	9/3/96	9 years, 11 months	10 years, 5 months
Liam	8/9/96	10 years, 0 months	10 years, 6 months
Heath	8/9/96	10 years, 0 months	10 years, 6 months
Nadia	8/2/96	10 years, 0 months	10 years, 6 months
Dan	7/25/96	10 years, 1 month	10 years, 7 months

NOTE: Classes are sometimes older or younger than average, depending on kindergarten cut-off dates and other factors. The students in this class, for example, are older than average.

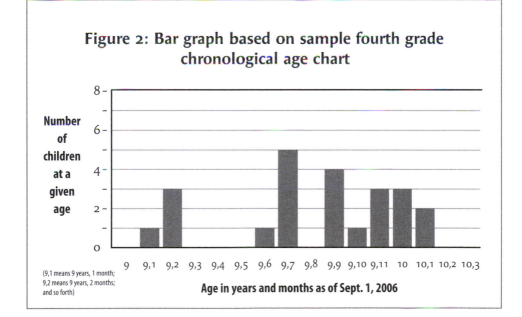

Figure 2: Bar graph based on sample fourth grade chronological age chart

Number of children at a given age

(9,1 means 9 years, 1 month; 9,2 means 9 years, 2 months; and so forth)

Age in years and months as of Sept. 1, 2006

Resources for Educators

———

The information in this book is foundational to the *Responsive Classroom* approach to teaching—a research-based education approach associated with greater teacher effectiveness, higher student achievement, and improved school climate. *Responsive Classroom* practices help educators build competencies in four interrelated domains: engaging academics, positive community, effective management, and developmentally responsive teaching. To learn more about the *Responsive Classroom* approach, see the following resources published by Center for Responsive Schools and available from www.responsiveclassroom.org • 800-360-6332.

Classroom Management: Set up and run a classroom in ways that enable the best possible teaching and learning.

Interactive Modeling: A Powerful Technique for Teaching Children
by Margaret Berry Wilson. 2012.

What Every Teacher Needs to Know, K–5 series, by Margaret Berry Wilson and Mike Anderson. 2010–2011. (Includes one book at each grade level.)

Teaching Children to Care: Classroom Management for Ethical and Academic Growth K–8, revised ed., by Ruth Sidney Charney. 2002.

Morning Meeting: Gather as a whole class each morning to greet each other, share news, and warm up for the day of learning ahead.

The Morning Meeting Book, 3rd ed., by Roxann Kriete and Carol Davis. 2014.

80 Morning Meeting Ideas for Grades K–2 by Susan Lattanzi Roser. 2012.

80 Morning Meeting Ideas for Grades 3–4 by Carol Davis. 2012.

Doing Language Arts in Morning Meeting: 150 Quick Activities That Connect to Your Curriculum by Jodie Luongo, Joan Riordan, and Kate Umstatter. 2015. (Includes a Common Core State Standards correlation guide.)

Doing Math in Morning Meeting: 150 Quick Activities That Connect to Your Curriculum by Andy Dousis and Margaret Berry Wilson. 2010. (Includes a Common Core State Standards correlation guide.)

Doing Science in Morning Meeting: 150 Quick Activities That Connect to Your Curriculum by Lara Webb and Margaret Berry Wilson. 2013. (Includes correlation guides to the Next Generation Science Standards and A Framework for K–12 Science Education, the basis for the standards.)

Morning Meeting Professional Development Kit. 2008.

Positive Teacher Language: Use words and tone as a tool to promote children's active learning, sense of community, and self-discipline.

The Power of Our Words: Teacher Language That Helps Children Learn, 2nd ed., by Paula Denton, EdD. 2014.

The Power of Our Words for Middle School: Teacher Language That Helps Students Learn. From *Responsive Classroom*. 2016.

Teacher Language for Engaged Learning: 4 Video Study Sessions. 2013.

Teacher Language Professional Development Kit. 2010.

Engaging Academics: Learn tools for effective teaching and making lessons lively, appropriately challenging, and purposeful to help children develop higher levels of motivation, persistence, and mastery of skills and content.

The Joyful Classroom: Practical Ways to Engage and Challenge Students K–6. From *Responsive Classroom.* 2016.

The Language of Learning: Teaching Students Core Thinking, Speaking, and Listening Skills by Margaret Berry Wilson. 2014.

Middle School Motivators: 22 Interactive Learning Structures. From *Responsive Classroom.* 2016.

Refocus and Recharge: 50 Brain Breaks for Middle Schoolers. From *Responsive Classroom.* 2016.

Teaching Discipline: Use practical strategies, such as rule creation and positive responses to misbehavior, to promote self-discipline in students and build a safe, calm, and respectful school climate.

Teasing, Tattling, Defiance and More: Positive Approaches to 10 Common Classroom Behaviors by Margaret Berry Wilson. 2013.

Rules in School: Teaching Discipline in the Responsive Classroom, 2nd ed., by Kathryn Brady, Mary Beth Forton, and Deborah Porter. 2011.

Responsive School Discipline: Essentials for Elementary School Leaders by Chip Wood and Babs Freeman-Loftis. 2011.

Teaching Discipline in the Classroom Professional Development Kit. 2011.

Foundation-Setting During the First Weeks of School: Take time in the critical first weeks of school to establish expectations, routines, a sense of community, and a positive classroom tone.

The First Six Weeks of School, 2nd ed. From *Responsive Classroom.* 2015.

Special Area Educators: Explore key *Responsive Classroom* practices adapted for a wide variety of special areas.

Responsive Classroom for Music, Art, PE, and Other Special Areas. From *Responsive Classroom.* August 2016.

Movement, Games, Songs, and Chants: Sprinkle quick, lively activities throughout the school day to keep students energized, engaged, and alert.

Closing Circles: 50 Activities for Ending the Day in a Positive Way by Dana Januszka and Kristen Vincent. 2012.

Energizers! 88 Quick Movement Activities That Refresh and Refocus by Susan Lattanzi Roser. 2009.

99 Activities and Greetings: Great for Morning Meeting . . . and other meetings, too! by Melissa Correa-Connolly. 2004.

Preventing Bullying at School: Use practical strategies throughout the day to create a safe, kind environment in which bullying is far less likely to take root.

How to Bullyproof Your Classroom by Caltha Crowe. 2012. (Includes bullying prevention lessons.)

Solving Behavior Problems With Children: Engage children in solving their behavior problems so they feel safe, challenged, and invested in changing.

Sammy and His Behavior Problems: Stories and Strategies from a Teacher's Year by Caltha Crowe. 2010.

Solving Thorny Behavior Problems: How Teachers and Students Can Work Together by Caltha Crowe. 2009.

Teasing, Tattling, Defiance and More: Positive Approaches to 10 Common Classroom Behaviors by Margaret Berry Wilson. 2013.

Working With Families: Hear parents' insights, help them understand the school's teaching approaches, and engage them as partners in their children's education.

Parents & Teachers Working Together by Carol Davis and Alice Yang. 2005.

Child and Adolescent Development: Understand common physical, social-emotional, cognitive, and language characteristics at each age, and adapt teaching to respond to developmental needs.

Child Development Pamphlet Series, K–8 (adapted from *Yardsticks*; available in English and Spanish). 2005 and 2006.

Adolescent Development Info Sheets (adapted from *Yardsticks*; 50 per pad). Available for 11-, 12-, 13-, and 14-year-olds. 2015.

Professional Development/Staff Meetings: Learn easy-to-use structures for getting the most out of your work with colleagues.

Energize Your Meetings! 35 Interactive Learning Structures for Educators. From *Responsive Classroom.* 2014.

Resources for Parents

Adolescence: The Survival Guide for Parents and Teenagers. Elizabeth Fenwick and Dr. Tony Smith. 1996.

Ages and Stages: Developmental Descriptions & Activities, Birth through Eight Years. Karen Miller. 1985.

A to Z Guide to Your Child's Behavior: A Parent's Easy and Authoritative Reference to Hundreds of Everyday Problems and Concerns From Birth to 12 Years. Compiled by the faculty of the Children's National Medical Center, under the direction of David Mrazek, M.D., and William Garrison, Ph.D., with Laura Elliott. 1993.

Between Form and Freedom: A Practical Guide to the Teenage Years. Betty Staley. 1988.

Black Children: Social, Educational, and Parental Environments. Harriette Pipes McAdoo, editor. 2002.

Black Children: Their Roots, Culture, and Learning Styles. Janice E. Hale-Benson. 1986.

Black Families. Harriet Pipes McAdoo, editor. 2007.

The Blessing of a Skinned Knee: Using Jewish Teachings to Raise Self-Reliant Children. Wendy Mogel, Ph.D. 2001.

Child Behavior. Frances L. Ilg, M.D., Louise Bates Ames, Ph.D., and Sidney M. Baker, M.D. 1981.

Childhood: A Multicultural View. Melvin Konner. 1993.

The Diary of Latoya Hunter: My First Year in Junior High. Latoya Hunter. 1992.

Resources for Parents

First Grade Takes a Test. Miriam Cohen. 2006. First published 1980.

How to Discipline Your Six to Twelve Year Old . . . Without Losing Your Mind. Jerry L. Wyckoff, Ph.D., and Barbara C. Unell. 1991.

How to Talk So Kids Can Learn at Home and in School. Adele Faber, Elaine Mazlish. 1995.

How to Talk So Kids Will Listen & Listen So Kids Will Talk. Adele Faber, Elaine Mazlish. 1980.

I Learn From Children. Caroline Pratt. 1970.

In a Different Voice. Carol Gilligan. 1982.

In My Room: Teenagers in Their Bedrooms. Adrienne Salinger. 1995.

Last Child in the Woods: Saving Our Children from Nature Deficit Disorder. Richard Louv. 2005.

The Magic Years. Selma H. Fraiberg. 1959.

Noah's Children: Restoring the Ecology of Childhood. Sara Stein. 2001.

Positive Discipline. Jane Nelsen. 2006.

Raising Black Children: Two Leading Psychiatrists Confront the Educational, Social and Emotional Problems Facing Black Children. James P. Comer, M.D., and Alvin F. Poussaint, M.D. 1992.

Reclaiming Childhood: Letting Children Be Children in Our Achievement-Oriented Society. William Crain. 2004.

Touchpoints: Your Child's Emotional and Behavioral Development. T. Berry Brazelton. 1992.

Your Child's Growing Mind. Jane M. Healy, Ph.D. 1987.

Your Ten to Fourteen Year Old. Louise Bates Ames, Ph.D., Frances L. Ilg, M.D., and Sidney Baker, M.D. 1988.

Some Favorite Books for Children at Different Ages

Thanks to the teachers of the Gill-Montague Regional School District in Massachusetts for contributing titles to these lists —Chip Wood

Choosing good children's books from among the many published each year can be a daunting task. This brief bibliography offers a few proven favorites, including some that have been popular with several generations of children. The books listed here fit the typical reading level for each age and also reflect common interests of children as they grow.

To discover more good books for children at each age, I strongly encourage parents and teachers to talk with school and public librarians. Attending school book fairs is another good way for parents and children to find books they can enjoy together.

Some Favorite Books for Children
AGES FOUR, FIVE, AND SIX

Abiyoyo. Pete Seeger. 1963.

And the Relatives Came. Cynthia Rylant. 1985.

A Is for Africa. Ifeoma Onyefulu. 1996.

Blueberries for Sal. Robert McCloskey. 1948.

Brave Charlotte. Anu Stohner. 2005.

Bringing the Rain to Kapiti Plain. Verna Aardema. 1981.

The Carrot Seed. Ruth Krauss. 1945.

The Caterpillar and the Polliwog. Jack Kent. 1985.

Cloudy with a Chance of Meatballs. Judi Barrett. 1978.

Emma Kate. Patricia Polacco. 2005.

First Grade Takes a Test. Miriam Cohen. 2006. First published 1980.

Frederick. Leo Lionni. 1967.

Go Dog Go. P.D. Eastman. 1961.

The Golden Rule. Ilene Cooper. 2007.

Henry and Mudge. Cynthia Rylant. 1987.

Ibis, A True Whale Story. John Himmelman. 1990.

If You Give a Mouse a Cookie. Laura Numeroff. 1985.

I-Spy series. Jean Marzollo. First title 1992.

It's About Cats. Gallimard Jeunesse. 1989.

A Kiss for Little Bear. Else H. Minarik. 1984.

Kitten's First Full Moon. Kevin Henkes. 2004.

The Little Mouse, the Red Ripe Strawberry, and the Hungry Bear. Don and Sudrey Wood. 1984.

The Lorax. Dr. Seuss. 1961.

Lost. Jay Cowley. 1981.

Lost Treasure of the Emerald Eye series. Geronimo Stilton. First title 2004.

My Weird School series. Dan Gutman. First title 2004.

No Fighting, No Biting. Else H. Minarik. 1978.

Owl Moon. Jane Yolen. 1987.

The Party. Jay Cowley. 1983.

Pearl's Pirates. Frank Asch. 1989.

The Problem with Chickens. Bruce McMillan. 2005.

The Rainbow Fish. Marcus Pfister. 1992.

Rainbow Goblins. Ulde Rico. 1978.

Roxaboxen. Alice Mclerran. 1991.

Sheep in a Jeep series. Nancy Shaw. First title 1988.

Skippyjon Jones (2005), *Skippyjon Jones in Mummy Trouble* (2006), *Skippyjon Jones in the Doghouse* (2007). Judy Schachner.

The Sneetches. Dr. Seuss. 1971.

A Trio for Grandpapa. Shulamith Oppenheim. 1974.

Two by Two. Barbara Reid. 1992.

The Vanishing Pumpkin. Tony Johnston. 1983.

The Very Hungry Caterpillar. Eric Carle. 1981.

Skin Again. Bell Hooks. 2004.

Some Favorite Books for Children
AGES SEVEN AND EIGHT

All About Sam. Lois Lowry. 1988.

The BFG. Roald Dahl. 1982.

The Boxcar Children series. Gertrude Chandler Warner. First title 1989.

Cat Heaven (1997), *Dog Heaven* (1995). Cynthia Rylant.

Catwings. Ursula K. LeGuin. 1988.

CDB! William Steig. 1987.

Charlie and the Chocolate Factory. Roald Dahl. 1964.

Charlotte's Web. E.B. White. 1953.

Dominic. William Steig. 1972.

Fantastic Mr. Fox. Roald Dahl. 1988.

George Washington's Socks. Elvira Woodruff. 1991.

The Haunted House. Dorothy Haas. 1988.

The Haunting of Grade Three. Grace Maccarone. 1984.

James and the Giant Peach. Roald Dahl. 1961.

Karen's Witch. Ann M. Martin. 1988.

The Little Mermaid. Deborah Hautzig. 1991.

The Littles and the Terrible Tiny Kid. John Peterson. 1993.

Matilda. Roald Dahl. 1988.

Midnight Express. Margaret Wetteren. 1990.

Mr. Putter and Tabby series. Cynthia Rylant. First title 1994.

My Father's Dragon, Elmer the Dragon, and *The Dragons of Blueland.* Ruth Stiles Gannett. 1987. First published 1948, 1950, 1951, respectively.

Mystery in the Night Woods. John Peterson. 1991.

Nate the Great series. Marjorie Sharmat. First title 1972.

The Rag Coat. Lauren Mills. 1991.

Ramona The Pest, Ramona Quimby: Age 8 and other Ramona books. Beverly Cleary. First title 1968.

Scary Stories. Alvin Schwartz. 1981.

The Story of Babe Ruth, Baseball's Greatest Legend. Lisa Eisenberg. 1990.

Stuart Little. E.B. White. 1945.

A Sweet Smell of Roses. Angela Johnson. 2005.

The Tree of Freedom. Rebecca Caudill. 1947.

23 Multicultural Tales to Tell. Pleasant de Spain. 1993.

The Witch and the Ring. Ruth Chew. 1992

Yuck Soup Story. Joy Cowley. 1986.

Zlateh the Goat and Other Stories. Isaac Bashevis Singer. 1984.

Some Favorite Books for Children
AGES NINE AND TEN

Anastasia Has The Answers. Lois Lowry. 1987.

Anastasia Krupnik. Lois Lowry. 1979.

The Brightest Light. Colleen O. McKenna. 1992.

The Chalk Doll. Charlotte Pomerantz. 1993.

Chronicles of Narnia. C.S. Lewis. 1953.

Double Play and other sports books. Matt Christopher. 1964.

Emily's Runaway Imagination. Beverly Cleary. 1985.

The Fourth Grade Wizards. Barthe DeClements. 1988.

From the Mixed-Up Files of Mrs. Basil E. Frankenweiler. E.L. Konigsburg. 1987.

The Great Brain at the Academy. John D. Fitzgerald. 1972.

Hare's Choice. Dennis Hamley. 1988.

The Indian in the Cupboard series. Lynn Reid Banks. First title 1987.

Jeremy Thatcher, Dragon Hatcher. Bruce Coville. 1991.

King of the Wind. Marguerite Henry. 1948.

Little House on the Prairie series. Laura Ingalls Wilder. First title 1932.

Mrs. Frisby and the Rats of NIMH. Robert C. O'Brien. 1971.

My Side of the Mountain. Jean Craighead George. 1959.

My Teacher Is an Alien. Bruce Coville. 1989.

Nothing's Fair in Fifth Grade. Barthe DeClements. 1990.

On the Far Side of the Mountain. Jean Craighead George. 1990.

Otis Spofford. Beverly Cleary. 1953.

Peter and the Wolf. Sergei Prokofiev. 1986.

Pippi Goes On Board. Astrid Lindgren. 1977.

Ralph S. Mouse. Beverly Cleary. 1982.

The Revenge of the Wizard's Ghost. John Bellairs. 1986.

Song of the Trees. Mildred D. Taylor. 1971.

Tales of a Fourth Grade Nothing. Judy Blume. 1972.

The Thirteen Clocks. James Thurber. 1978. First published 1950.

Volcano. Meryl Siegman. 1987.

Walk When the Moon Is Full. Frances Hamerstrom. 1975.

Some Favorite Books for Children
AGES ELEVEN AND TWELVE

A Connecticut Yankee in King Arthur's Court. Mark Twain. 1983. First published 1889.

The Adventures of Tom Sawyer. Mark Twain. 1983. First published 1876.

Black Beauty: The Autobiography of a Horse. Anna Sewell. 1990. First published 1877.

Blood Root. Doug Hobbie. 1991.

The Book of Three. Lloyd Alexander. 1964.

The Borning Room. Paul Fleishman. 1991.

Bridge to Terabithia. Katherine Paterson. 1977.

Charlie and the Chocolate Factory. Roald Dahl. 1964.

Children of the Wolf. Jane Yolen. 1984.

Comet in Moominland. Tove Jansson. 1991.

The Devil's Arithmetic. Jane Yolen. 1988.

Dragon of the Lost Sea. Laurence Yep. 1994.

Dragon Singer. Anne McCaffrey. 1978.

The Egypt Game. Zilpha Snyder. 1967.

The Friendship (1987), *The Gold Cadillac* (1987). Mildred Taylor.

Frightful's Mountain. Jean Craighead George. 1999.

Ghosts I Have Been. Richard Peck. 1992.

The Girl on the Outside. Mildred Pitts Walker. 1993.

Harriet the Spy. Louise Fitzhugh. 1964.

The Hobbit. J.R.R. Tolkien. 1984.

A Horse Called Holiday. Frances Wilbur. 1992.

The Journey Back. Johanna Reiss. 1976.

The Little Prince. Antoine de Saint-Exupery. 1971.

Number the Stars. Lois Lowry. 1990.

Redwall series. Brian Jacques. First title 1986.

The Riddle Master of Hed. Patricia A. McKillip. 1978.

The Search for Delicious. Natalie Babbitt. 1969.

A Sending of Dragons. Jane Yolen. 1987.

A Single Shard. Linda Sue Park. 2001.

Sixth Grade Secrets. Louis Sachar. 1987.

Snow Treasure. Marie Mcswigan. 1942.

The Summer of the Falcon. Jean Craighead George. 1990. First published 1962.

A Swiftly Tilting Planet. Madeleine L'Engle. 1978.

The Tale of Despereaux: Being the Story of a Mouse, a Princess, Some Soup and a Spool of Thread. Kate Dicamillo. 2003.

The Truth About Sixth Grade. Colleen O. McKenna. 1991.

The Upstairs Room. Johanna Reiss. 1972.

The Vampire's Promise. Caroline B. Cooney. 1993.

Witches. Roald Dahl. 1988.

The Wizard in the Hall. Lloyd Alexander. 1975.

A Wrinkle in Time. Madeleine L'Engle. 1962.

Some Favorite Books for Children
AGES THIRTEEN AND FOURTEEN

Allegra Maud Goldman. Edith Konecky. 1976.

Annie John. Jamaica Kincaid. 1986.

Anpao. Jamake Highwater. 1992.

Arm of the Starfish. Madeleine L'Engle. 1980.

Bread and Roses Too. Katherine Paterson. 2006.

The Chocolate War. Robert Cormier. 1974.

David and Jonathan. Cynthia Voight. 1992.

A Day No Pigs Would Die. Robert Newton Peck. 1972.

The Diary of Adrian Mole. Sue Townsend. 1982.

The Diary of Latoya Hunter. Latoya Hunter. 1992.

Fallen Angel. Walter Dean Myers. 1989.

The Farthest Shore. Ursula LeGuin. 1984.

The Giver. Lois Lowry. 1994.

Good-Bye and Keep Cold. Jenny Davis. 1987.

House of Dies Drear. Virginia Hamilton. 1968.

The House on Mango Street. Sandra Cisneros. 1991.

I Heard the Owl Call My Name. Margaret Craven. 1980.

Make Lemonade. Virginia Euwer Wolff. 1994.

Meet the Austins. Madeleine L'Engle. 1981.

Missing May. Cynthia Rylant. 2005.

The Monument. Gary Paulsen. 1991.

Never Cry Wolf. Farley Mowat. 1983.

Nothing But the Truth. Avi. 1993.

The Outsiders. S.E. Hinton. 1967.

The Ransom of Mercy Carter. Caroline B. Cooney. 2001.

Roll of Thunder, Hear My Cry. Mildred Taylor.

The Runner. Cynthia Voight. 1985.

Scorpions. Walter Dean Myers. 1988.

A Stranger in the Kingdom. Howard Frank Mosher. 1990.

Watership Down. Richard Adams. 1972.

About the Author

For forty years, Robert (Chip) Wood has worked with children from preschool through eighth grade as a classroom teacher, teaching principal, and teacher educator. After studying at the Gesell Institute of Human Development early in his career, Chip made developmentally based teaching the center of his educational practice. His core belief: Knowing what children at each age are developmentally capable of doing physically, socially, emotionally, and cognitively enables respectful, successful teaching of all children— no matter their life circumstances or cultural background. Chip is a co-founder of Northeast Foundation for Children (now Center for Responsive Schools) and served as principal of Sheffield Elementary School in Turners Falls, Massachusetts, and director of curriculum, instruction, and professional development for the Gill Montague Regional School District in Massachusetts.

About the Publisher

Center for Responsive Schools, Inc., a not-for-profit educational organization, is the developer of *Responsive Classroom*®, a research-based education approach associated with greater teacher effectiveness, higher student achievement, and improved school climate. *Responsive Classroom* practices help educators build competencies in four interrelated domains: engaging academics, positive community, effective management, and developmentally responsive teaching. We offer the following resources for educators:

Professional Development Services

- Workshops for K–8 educators (locations around the country and internationally)
- On-site consulting services to support implementation
- Resources for site-based study
- Annual conferences for K–8 educators

Publications and Resources

- Books on a wide variety of *Responsive Classroom* topics
- Professional development kits for school-based study
- Free newsletter for educators
- Extensive library of free articles on our website

For details, contact:

Responsive Classroom®

Center for Responsive Schools, Inc.
85 Avenue A, P.O. Box 718
Turners Falls, Massachusetts 01376-0718

800-360-6332 ■ www.responsiveclassroom.org
info@responsiveclassroom.org